Success guides

Standard Grade
French

✗ Colin Hamilton ✗

Text © 2005 Colin Hamilton

Design and layout © 2005 Leckie & Leckie

Cover image © Getty Images

06/270208

978-1-84372-282-3

Published by

Leckie & Leckie Ltd, 3rd Floor, 4 Queen Street, Edinburgh EH2 1JE

tel. 0131 220 6831   fax. 0131 225 9987

enquiries@leckieandleckie.co.uk   www.leckieandleckie.co.uk

Special thanks to

Lisa Albarracin & Betty Templeton (content review),
Andrew Elkerton (illustration), Chantal Hamill (indexing),
Ken Vail Graphic Design & The Partnership Publishing Solutions (design and page make-up),
Caleb Rutherford (cover design),Tracy Traynor (copy-editing), Angela Wigmore (proofreading),
Phil Booth (sound engineering), Kate Chaillet and Andrew Slater (French speakers).

A CIP Catalogue record for this book is available from the British Library.

Leckie & Leckie is a division of Huveaux plc.

Contents

Personal Language

Tourist Language

Problems

Writing and Speaking

Foreword

Bonjour à tous!

Here are a few words of introduction to your *Standard Grade French Success Guide*, in order to help you get the most benefit from it.

If you use it well, this book will improve your skills and knowledge. To help you do this I have covered the essential areas of the Standard Grade course (that is, major topic areas with important vocabulary and grammatical explanations, followed by reading and listening exercises) so that your French will progress as you work your way through the text. Extended work is labelled throughout to help you push yourself.

You will also find practical help throughout on exam and assessment matters. In addition, your teacher will probably give you exam practice using Past Papers. But the best way to prepare for your exams is to *improve* your French. It's that simple!

You will get more from your study by understanding what some of the different features of this book are for:

- The Quick Test sections are either marked with this icon for straightforward comprehension questions, or with

  for more imaginative exercises (these are intended to be more challenging).

- This icon identifies material important to consider for folio writing.

- 'A step further', or

  'Credit', signify that this material is very difficult, but still highly relevant to the strongest pupils at this level.

- *20* This CD icon beside the listening exercises refers to a listening track on the CD.

I have included some topics with lots of challenging vocabulary: for example the **Environment** and **One world** topics. It's amazing how these areas find their way into Credit reading and listening every year now. Enjoy stretching your knowledge!

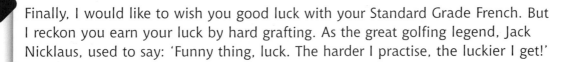

Finally, I would like to wish you good luck with your Standard Grade French. But I reckon you earn your luck by hard grafting. As the great golfing legend, Jack Nicklaus, used to say: 'Funny thing, luck. The harder I practise, the luckier I get!'

Colin Hamilton

Course summary

Your *Success Guide* deals with the main topics of the Standard Grade French course. It divides them up in this way:

Personal Language	Tourist Language	Problems
Self	Where I live	Relationships
Family	Transport	Health issues
Hobbies	Holidays	Environment
Education	Eating out	One world

Nearly everything that comes up in your Standard Grade exams in Reading and Listening – and that you do in your Speaking and Writing Assessments – can be linked to these topics: they are covered in the first three chapters of this book – **Personal Language**, **Tourist Language** and **Problems**. Topics not falling into these categories (numbers, times and dates), are grouped together for handy reference in the **Some basic language** section at the back of the book.

For reference, here is a list of all the topics you need to cover for Standard Grade:
- Personal information given / asked for in polite language
- Members of family, friends and friendship, physical and character description, interpersonal problems and relationships
- Parts of the body, illnesses / accidents
- Making appointments
- Houses / rooms and the ideal house
- Comparison of routine and lifestyles in Scotland and in France / other French-speaking countries
- Life in the future; past and future events (in routine)
- Comparison of education system with that of France / other French-speaking countries
- Leisure, sports and health issues: healthy eating, exercise, drugs
- TV, film and music
- Other food issues
- Restaurants / menus, making arrangements
- Giving simple and complex directions
- Tourist information, comparison of town / country, helping the environment
- Changing money
- Negotiating transactional problems
- Jobs / Working and studying
- Relative merits of jobs
- Work experience
- Future employment
- Travel information
- Travel plans

- Relative merits of different means of transport
- Comparisons between different countries
- Weather
- Future holidays
- Ideal holidays
- Past holidays

As you'll see, in our coverage of the topics we've grouped many of them together, because learning in context actually makes your revision easier.

In addition, we've given verbs special attention, as getting tenses right is of particular importance at Standard Grade. The chapter on **Writing and Speaking** focuses on the past, present and future tenses, to help you master the structures you need to be confident on all the Standard Grade topics.

Good luck!

Assessment summary

Assessment at a glance

Standard Grades are all marked according to these grades and levels:

Grades	Levels
1–2	Credit
3–4	General
5–6	Foundation

Reading and Speaking

Reading and Speaking grades are given twice the weight of Listening and Writing (as they are considered the most important by the exam board), and therefore count double when your Overall Grade is made up as an average:

Skills	Weighting
Reading	2
Listening	1
Speaking	2
Writing	1

Here's an example of how this might work in practice:

Skills	Grades	Overall Grade
Reading	3 (so, 3 × 2) → 6	6 + 2 + 4 + 1 = 13 divided by 4 = 3.25
Listening	2	
Speaking	2 (so, 2 × 2) → 4	
Writing	1	

So, the Overall Grade here is grade 3.

Assessment in detail

Reading and Listening Exams

You will sit both Reading and Listening papers on the same two levels. If you are a Credit candidate, then you'll do both Credit and General papers. A Foundation candidate will do Foundation and General papers.

Reading and Listening grades are based purely on the external exams in the May or June of S4. These are made up of a mixture of the Standard Grade topics, so you will need to revise **all** of your vocabulary thoroughly, and not just certain topics.

Reading

The **Reading** papers (F – 45 minutes; G – 45 minutes; C – 60 minutes) allow you to use a dictionary. The various questions are often totally unrelated to one another. Questions and answers are all in English.

Listening

In the **Listening** papers, no dictionaries are allowed. These exams are much shorter (F – 25 minutes max.; G – 25 minutes max.; C – 30 minutes max.), and are usually about a visit to France, with all the questions are about various things that happen in that situation, but covering many different topic areas. All questions and answers are in English. The questions are all introduced in English, and then you hear the actual French three times.

Speaking

This grade is based on the average grade of your three speaking assessments, usually in S4 (although in theory they could come from S3). Speaking assessments are carried out in school by your French teacher, and sometimes the way they are conducted and graded is checked by the exam board. Your speaking assessments will normally be finished by February or March in S4.

You will do three types of speaking assessment:

- A prepared talk (max. 2 minutes; three headings of max. of three words each can be used), e.g. *Les grandes vacances.*
- A conversation (max. 5 minutes; with teacher or another pupil), e.g. *Mes passe-temps.*

- A role-play (max. 5 minutes; with teacher or another pupil). This role-play is either *transactional* or *vocational*, so it's about exchanging information or dealing with a particular 'official' situation, e.g. Transactional: *Booking into a hotel*; Vocational: *Working in a tourist information office.*

Bear in mind what examiners are looking for in your speaking assessments, that is:

- Establishing contact
- Exchanging or presenting information
- Explaining and instructing
- Expressing opinion and reasons
- Expressing understanding.

You need to try to cover these over the three pieces.

Your speaking assessments are done at the end of a particular topic in French, and you will be given specific instructions by your teacher, along with adequate time and support to prepare. Plenty of practice at home will also be necessary in order to memorise properly. Have a look at the examples in the chapter on **Writing and Speaking**.

Writing

The writing part of your Standard Grade consists of your three best pieces done under test conditions over S3 and S4. These are sent off to the exam board for them to mark in February or March of S4. Your teacher will probably let you know whether you are getting a Credit or a General or a Foundation level in your Folio pieces, but remember it is the actual exam board (or SQA) who mark them.

You can choose, possibly with a little direction from your teacher, the titles of your Folio essays. Remember, it is the *quality of writing* which counts, so the titles should represent areas of French which you are confident you can write well on. Bear in mind also the normal word counts (which are **only guidelines**):

- Foundation: 25–50 words
- General: 50–100 words
- Credit: 100–200 words.

It is best to have a fairly general title, but write specific bullet points of things you intend to include in the piece. This will help give you a structure, and this in turn makes it easier to draft and memorise. (Remember, if you are using bullet points as a memory aid in the actual test, the teacher must agree to the wording of these!)

e.g.   *Le week-end dernier*

- Where I went last weekend
- What I did on Saturday (played hockey; watched TV; met up with friends)
- Sunday morning – walk

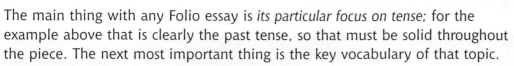

The main thing with any Folio essay is *its particular focus on tense;* for the example above that is clearly the past tense, so that must be solid throughout the piece. The next most important thing is the key vocabulary of that topic.

Remember what examiners are looking for in your Folio, that is the ability to present:

- Information
- Opinions
- Reasons.

Top Tip
The dictionary is only really to be used to check the spelling or gender of a word, not to provide you with entirely new or unprepared vocabulary in the test! See the examples in the chapter on **Writing and Speaking**.

Self 1

Basic vocabulary

General intro

Salut!	Hi!
Bonjour!	Hello!
Je m'appelle …	My name is …
J'ai quatorze / quinze ans.	I'm 14 / 15 (years old).
Mon anniversaire, c'est le douze juillet.	My birthday is 12 July.
J'habite à … en Ecosse.	I live in … in Scotland.
… se trouve dans …	… is in …
le nord	the north
le sud	the south
l'est	the east
l'ouest	the west

Physical

Je suis très / assez …	I'm very / quite …
grand / grande	tall
petit / petite	small
gros / grosse	fat
mince	slim

J'ai …	I've got …
les cheveux blonds / bruns / noirs	blond / brown / black hair
les yeux bleus / verts	blue / green eyes

Character

Je suis …	I am …

sportif / sportive	sporty
sérieux / sérieuse	serious
intelligent / intelligente	intelligent
paresseux / paresseuse	lazy
drôle	funny
amusant / amusante	funny
sympa	nice

Extended vocabulary

General

La date de mon anniversaire, c'est le …	My birthday is on the …
Je suis écossais / écossaise.	I'm Scottish.

Physical

J'ai …	I've got …
les yeux marron / gris	brown / grey eyes
les cheveux roux	red hair
les cheveux teints	dyed hair
les cheveux longs / courts	long / short hair
les cheveux bouclés / frisés / raides	curly / curly / straight hair

Je suis …	I'm …
absolument	absolutely
complètement	completely
tout à fait	totally

fort / forte	strong, tough
costaud	strong, tough
robuste	strong, tough
beau / belle	good-looking
laid / laide	ugly

Je porte des lunettes.	I wear glasses.
Je suis de taille moyenne.	I'm average height.

Character

À mon avis …	In my opinion …
je suis …	I am …
en général	generally
plutôt	rather
toujours	always
vraiment	really

actif / active	active
agréable	pleasant
aimable	friendly
gentil / gentille	kind
marrant / marrante	amusing
sensible	sensitive
sensé / sensée	sensible

Mais, de temps en temps, je suis …	But, from time to time, I am …
méchant / méchante	naughty
timide	shy
égoïste	selfish
impatient / impatiente	impatient
insupportable	unbearable

Quick Test

Translate the following sentences into English:

1 *Elle est assez grande et mince.*
2 *J'ai les cheveux bruns et les yeux verts.*
3 *Il est sérieux mais amusant.*
4 *Je suis tout à fait impatiente.*
5 *Ma mère est vraiment sensible.*

Quick Test

Draw a long straight line across a blank page: to the left of the line, write down negative adjectives, to the right positive (with the more extreme words on the far left or far right, the less extreme closer to the centre). See if you can come up with thirty words, appropriately placed. Decide first whether you are going to use masculine or feminine adjectives.

Self 2

Basic grammar

Essential details

- *Je m'appelle …*   My name is …
  Note the spelling: *appelle*.

- *J'**ai** quinze ans.*   I'm 15 (years old).
  Note that the French say 'I *have* 15 years' (it's not *Je **suis** 15 ans*).

- *le douze juillet*   (on) 12 July
  Most dates use cardinal numbers (12, 13, etc., not 12th, 13th, etc.). See the Top Tip.
  Months have no capital.

- *j'ai*   I have
  je suis   I am

- Many adjectives add an –e in the feminine. This often affects the sound of the word.
  *intelligent**e***
  *amusant**e***
  *gross**e***
  *laid**e***
  *fort**e***

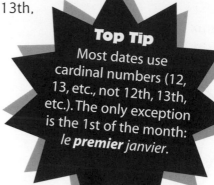

Top Tip
Most dates use cardinal numbers (12, 13, etc., not 12th, 13th, etc.). The only exception is the 1st of the month: *le **premier** janvier.*

Extended grammar

Trickier details

- Adjectives for hair and eyes remain the same, whether their owner is male or female.
  *Il a les cheveux **blonds** et **courts** et les yeux **verts**.*
  *Elle a les cheveux **blonds** et **courts** et les yeux **verts**.*

- Some adjectives do not change in the feminine form.
  sensible
  agréable
  aimable
  sympa
  égoïste
  Some change in spelling but not in pronunciation.
  sensé(e)

- You need a wide range of verbs to describe yourself in greater detail. Learning the following will give you a good start. Note the useful negative construction *ne … pas*.

*Je m'**appelle** Jon.*
*J'**ai** quatorze ans.*
*J'**habite** Édimbourg.*
*Je **suis** écossais.*
*Je **suis** grand et sportif.*
*J'**ai** les cheveux blonds et bouclés.*
*J'**ai** les yeux marron.*
*J'**ai** un frère.*
*Je **n'ai pas** d'animal.*
*J'**adore** le rugby.*
*Je **déteste** les examens.*
*J'**aime** écouter la radio.*
*Je **n'aime pas** faire les travaux ménagers.*
*Je **joue** au golf.*
*Je **fais** de la natation.*

Quick Test

Describe yourself in this way.

Self 3

Exercise 1

Now complete this grid to test your knowledge and understanding of the 'Self' topic. It will take you beyond the *Success Guide* and back to your own course notes from school!

Top Tip
All you need, in order to describe yourself, is to change the details in each of these phrases. Brand new sentences are not needed! Try it!

French	English
les cheveux roux	
les yeux marron	
les cheveux raides	
Je suis de taille moyenne.	
Je suis assez costaud.	
Je ne suis pas très fort.	
sympa	
sensible	
égoïste	
J'ai quinze ans.	
Je suis anglais.	
Je n'ai pas de frère.	
J'habite Glasgow.	
C'est dans l'ouest.	
Mon anniversaire, c'est le deux mars.	
	I've got blue eyes.
	I've got black hair.
	I'm quite small and thin.
	I'm generally friendly.
	I'm rarely mean.
	I'm sometimes shy.

Top Tip
Exam skills: In listening exercises it is very important to listen out for the small details, as you will not score full marks for incomplete answers. Minor details are often expressed through the adverbs we've come across in this section: *assez, très, complètement, tout à fait* and *absolument*. So check you know their meaning!

Exercise 2

CREDIT

1 — Read and listen to this description by a French actor of the 'baddie' he plays in his most recent film. He's quite an unpleasant chap!

- Alors, tout le monde, dans mon dernier film que j'ai tourné, je suis assez méchant!

- D'abord, je suis toujours en colère! La musique classique me rend fâché!

- Et en plus, de temps en temps, je suis tout à fait désagréable!

- Par exemple, je suis souvent violent (je suis très costaud, moi)!

- Je mesure deux mètres, alors je suis vraiment très grand ...

- ... et je pèse quatre-vingt-dix kilos parce que je suis assez gros (j'adore les glaces au chocolat et les pizzas)!

- Tout le monde dit que suis un peu laid. Ce n'est pas vrai, je vous le dis, je suis HORRIBLEMENT laid, avec un ENORME nez et de SUPER-GRANDES oreilles. Et je suis aussi plein de boutons! Absolument affreux! Yeuch!

- Ma mère dit toujours que je suis bête, et c'est vrai (j'étais vraiment nul en maths à l'école)!

- Ce que j'aime? Et bien, j'adore les rats, les gangsters, les crapauds, les gangsters, les hôpitaux, les gangsters ...

- Ce que je n'aime pas? Alors, moi, je déteste les femmes charmantes, les belles robes, les petits bébés ... oui, je trouve tout ça insupportable!

- Heh! heh! heh! Mon nom est Cassepieds, Richard Cassepieds ... enchanté de faire votre connaissance!

Use the information either to draw a poster of Richard or note down in English all you now know about him!

Quick Test C

True or False?

1 Classical music makes him angry. ☐

2 He is under 2 metres tall. ☐

3 He weighs 86 kilos. ☐

4 He struggled with maths at school. ☐

5 He loves toads. ☐

6 He adores babies. ☐

7 He is never violent. ☐

8 He has huge ears and a big nose. ☐

Quick Test i

Can you now describe the detective who has the job of catching Richard Cassepieds? He is all the things the gangster is not – you'll need to use very different vocabulary!

Family 1

Basic vocabulary

Family

Voici …	Here is …
mon frère	my brother
mon cousin (m)	my cousin (male)
mon père	my father
mon oncle	my uncle
mon grand-père	my grandfather
ma sœur	my sister
ma cousine (f)	my cousin (female)
ma mère	my mother
ma tante	my aunt
ma grand-mère	my grandmother
Voici …	Here are …
mes parents	my parents
mes grands-parents	my grandparents

Work

Il / Elle va à l'école.	He / She goes to school.
Il / Elle travaille dans …	He / She works in …
un bureau	an office
un supermarché	a supermarket
un magasin	a shop
un centre sportif	sports centre
une entreprise	a company
une banque	a bank
une bibliothèque	a library
Il / Elle est …	He / She is …
professeur	a teacher
médecin / docteur	a doctor
dentiste	a dentist
journaliste	a journalist

vétérinaire	a vet
chef	a chef / a boss
secrétaire	a secretary
directeur / directrice	a primary school headteacher / a (company) director
patron / patronne	a boss
facteur / factrice	a postman
maçon / maçonne	a builder

Top Tip
In French, you don't say 'a' teacher or 'an' electrician – simply 'he is teacher' or 'she is electrician'.

infirmier / infirmière	a nurse
programmeur / programmeuse	a computer programmer
mécanicien / mécanicienne	a mechanic
électricien / électricienne	an electrician
commerçant / commerçante	a sales person
homme / femme d'affaires	a businessman
vendeur / vendeuse	a shop assistant

Extended vocabulary

Family

mon demi-frère	my half-brother / step-brother
mon frère aîné / cadet	my elder / younger brother
mon frère jumeau	my twin brother
mon beau-père	my step-father / father-in-law
mon copain	my friend / boyfriend
mon petit ami	my boyfriend
mon fiancé	my fiancé
mon mari	my husband
mon époux (m)	my spouse
mon fils	my son

ma demi-sœur	my half-sister / step-sister
ma sœur aînée / cadette	my elder / younger sister
ma sœur jumelle	my twin sister
ma belle-mère	my step-mother / mother-in-law
ma copine	my friend / girlfriend
ma petite amie	my girlfriend
ma fiancée	my fiancée

ma femme	my wife
mon épouse* (f)	my spouse
ma fille	my daughter

* Note that it's *mon* with a feminine noun starting with a vowel.

Work

Il / Elle va …	He / She goes …
à l'école primaire	to primary school
à l'école secondaire	to secondary school
au collège	to *collège* [French secondary school up to 16]
au lycée	to *lycée* [French secondary school 16–18]

Il / Elle travaille …	He / She works …
avec les jeunes	with young people
chez MacDo	at McDonald's
dans un laboratoire	in a lab
dans une usine	in a factory
dans une maison des jeunes	in a youth club

Il /Elle est …	He / She is …
pompier / pompière	a fireman
fermier / fermière	a farmer
boucher / bouchère	a butcher
boulanger / boulangère	a baker
décorateur / décoratrice	a decorator
dessinateur / dessinatrice	a designer
ouvrier / ouvrière	a worker
employé / employée	an employee
étudiant / étudiante	a student
chômeur / chômeuse	unemployed

Quick Test

Can you remember a job beginning with:

b   d   p   f   é

Can you find the feminine for these family members:

- *copain*
- *mari*
- *époux*
- *fiancé*

Now write in the meanings next to the words above. Use a dictionary for any jobs you're not sure of, and then memorise the French. Write out as many as you can recall in French.

Family 2

Basic grammar

My

'my' has three different forms in French:

mon – with a male member of the family, e.g. **mon** *frère*

ma – with a female member of the family, e.g. **ma** *sœur*

mes – with more than one person, e.g. **mes** *parents*

Remember that it doesn't matter *who's talking*.

> *Je m'appelle Marc.*
> *Voici* **mon frère***, Luc.*
> *Voici* **ma sœur** *aînée, Marie.*
> *Voici* **mes parents***.*

> *Salut! C'est moi, Sophie!*
> *Voici* **mon père** *et* **ma mère***.*
> *Et voici* **mes grands-parents***:*
> *ils sont très gentils.*

Useful verbs

> *Marie* **a** *vingt ans.*
> *Elle* **habite** *au centre-ville avec son copain.*
> *Elle* **travaille** *à l'hôpital, comme infirmière.*
> *Elle* **joue** *du piano depuis dix ans.*

> *Mon père* **est** *travailleur.*
> *Il* **va** *souvent au marché.*
> *Tous les dimanches, il* **fait** *du vélo.*
> *Il* **aime lire** *aussi.*

Most verbs with *il / elle* end in –e, but some don't.

Note also that if you use two verbs together in the present tense, the second is in the infinitive – *aime lire*.

For more information on verbs see **Tenses 1** on pages 84–6.

Jobs – male or female

Finally, you need to note that many jobs have two different forms, depending on whether they are done by a man or a woman:

Mon oncle est **infirmier***.*	*Ma tante est* **infirmière***.*
Mon frère est **vendeur***.*	*Ma sœur est* **vendeuse***.*
Mon copain est **mécanicien***.*	*Ma copine est* **mécanicienne***.*

Some jobs don't change:

Hugo est **professeur***.*	*Maryline est* **professeur***.*
Jean-Paul voudrait devenir **astronaute***.*	*Amélie est* **astronaute***.*

Extended grammar

Your, his / her

You've already had a look at the words for 'my' in French. Well – good news! The words for 'your', 'his' and 'her' all follow the **same pattern**. Remember: the form used depends on who is being referred to and not on the speaker.

ton *frère*	your brother
ta *sœur*	your sister
tes *parents*	your parents
son *frère*	his / her brother
sa *sœur*	his / her sister
ses *parents*	his / her parents

Imperfect tense

We've spent a lot of time talking about the **present** tense – how and what people are **these days**.

However, when we want to describe **how things were** *or* **used to be**, then we need to use another tense called the **imperfect**.

Take a look at the verbs below, which are all in the imperfect tense (and in bold). Granny is talking to you about the good old days …

In the imperfect tense, the ending for *il / elle* (he / she) is *–ait,* and for *ils / elles* (they) is *–aient*.

For more information on how to form the imperfect tense see **Tenses 3** on pages 90–93.

Top Tip

It is important to be able to recognise the imperfect tense in listening and reading exercises, as it usually indicates when people are describing the past or how things used to be. Remember that in listening the endings for 'he' and 'they' ('*il*' and '*ils*') sound the same, e.g. in *il jouait* and *ils jouaient* both have the 'eh' sound at the end. So you need to listen out for other clues, such as names, proper nouns (*mes parents*, etc.) numbers of people concerned, and other details – in short, the context or situation in question.

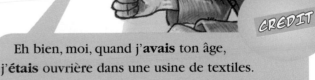

Quick Test C

Match up!

1	*ses frères*	a	your mother
2	*ton ami*	b	his / her brother
3	*ta mère*	c	his / her parents
4	*son oncle*	d	his / her uncle
5	*ses parents*	e	his / her brothers
6	*son frère*	f	your friend

Eh bien, moi, quand j'**avais** ton âge, j'**étais** ouvrière dans une usine de textiles.

Le travail **était** très difficile, car il **faisait** toujours très chaud dans l'usine, et on **travaillait** toute la journée …

Mes deux frères, Bernard et Bazire, n'**aimaient** pas ce genre de travail, et **préféraient** rester à la ferme. Ils **jouaient** souvent le week-end au football ou **faisaient** des promenades en bateau … Le lundi, ils **allaient** au marché pour les achats. Ah oui, la vie **était** bien difficile, tu sais!

Quick Test i

Can you divide the jobs into various types? Those which don't change from masculine to feminine, those which add an *–e* in the feminine, etc.?

Family 3

Exercise 1

To test yourself on the main grammar and vocabulary points, complete the grids below:

My ...	Family member
mon	frère
	grand-père
	demi-sœur
	copain
	petite amie
	parents
His ...	
sa	mère
	tante
	oncle
Her ...	
ses	copines
	amis
	grands-parents

Male jobs	Female jobs
programmeur d'ordinateur	
vendeur dans un grand magasin	
	professeur de sciences naturelles
	secrétaire au lycée
directeur d'une entreprise	

Present	Imperfect	English
Elle travaille au centre-ville.		
Il va au collège.		
Ils habitent Strasbourg.		
	Il était fermier.	
	Ils avaient un magasin.	
	Ma mère jouait du piano.	
		They work abroad.

Exercise 2

2 — Read through and listen to this description of a French family.

Count Malfoi is taking you through the corridors of his ancestral home, pointing out the characters behind the portraits hanging on the walls ...

Look at the grid following the text. Note the information for each member of the family.

CREDIT

'Eh bien, mon cher ami, vous voulez écouter l'histoire personnelle de ma famille, n'est-ce pas?

Alors, voici mon grand-père Victor, qui est mort en 1996 à l'âge de quatre-vingt-neuf ans. Il était très grand et mince, avec une longue barbe grise et des moustaches ENORMES. Grand-père était très riche mais généreux ... Il travaillait comme directeur d'une banque nationale à Paris.'

Top Tip
Note down any new vocabulary from this reading / listening text, arranging these new words into types, such as adjectives, verbs, etc.

'Et maintenant, ma grand-mère Marie-Antoinette. Elle était vraiment belle, n'est-ce pas, ma grand-mère? Elle est morte il y a dix ans, quand elle n'avait que quatre-vingt-deux ans, donc elle n'était pas très vieille. Ma grand-mère venait de la Roumanie où elle était mannequin célèbre avant de devenir danseuse. Mes grands-parents se sont rencontrés à un spectacle … '

CREDIT

'Voici mon père, Gérard. Il a soixante ans. Il est à la retraite maintenant, mais il était homme d'affaires pour une grande société américaine pendant trente ans. Mon père est très sévère et autoritaire, mais il est aussi aimable et compréhensif de temps en temps. Il est assez gros, avec les cheveux courts et bouclés et il porte des lunettes.'

CREDIT

'Et finalement, permettez-moi de vous présenter ma mère, la belle Eloise. Elle est d'origine espagnole, car elle est née à Madrid en 1958. Quand elle était jeune, elle était comédienne de théâtre, et tout le monde l'adorait! Ma mère a les yeux marron et les cheveux longs et bruns. Elle est sensible et charmante avec un sens de l'humour – elle adore faire des plaisanteries à la maison quand nous avons des invités!'

CREDIT

'Alors, mon cher ami Ludovic, j'espère que vous avez apprécié ma petite description domestique … !'

You can limit yourself to three boxes each time if you wish!

Family member	Age	Physical description	Character	Job	Other details

Top Tip
There is a crucial difference between some written and spoken words in French. Most of the time consonants are silent; you don't hear them but only read them. Listen to exercise 2 and circle the silent letters.

Quick Test C

Write out these statements under the correct name:

a quite fat

b died ten years ago

c worked for a big American company

d has a sense of humour

e was born in Spain

Quick Test i

Can you make a list of present tense versus imperfect tense verbs?

Hobbies 1

Basic vocabulary

Places you go to

J'aime aller …	I like to go …
en ville	into town
voir mes ami(e)s	to see my friends
au cinéma	to the cinema
au théâtre	to the theatre
au club des jeunes	to the youth club
au centre de loisirs	to the leisure centre
au stade de football	to the football stadium
au parc	to the park
à la patinoire	to the ice-rink
à la piscine	to the swimming pool
à la maison des jeunes	to the youth club
à la disco	to the disco
aux magasins	to the shops
aux concerts	to the concerts
aux boums / fêtes	to the parties

Hobbies

Mon passe-temps préféré, c'est …	My favourite hobby is …
Mes passe-temps préférés sont …	My favourite hobbies are …
J'aime …	I like …
J'adore …	I love …
Je n'aime pas …	I don't like …
Je déteste …	I hate …
le rugby	rugby
le foot	football
le basket	basketball
le volley	volleyball
le hand	handball

le judo	judo
le jogging / footing	jogging
le karaté	karate
la cuisine	cooking
la photographie	photography
la musique pop	pop music
la planche à voile	windsurfing
les ordinateurs	computers
les jeux vidéos	video games
les jeux d'ordinateur	computer games
les promenades en vélo	bike rides

Things to do

Ça m'intéresse de faire …	I'm interested in …
du shopping / les magasins	going shopping
du cyclisme / vélo	cycling
du ski	skiing
du patin	skating
de la natation	swimming
de l'équitation	horse-riding
des promenades	going for walks

Sport

J'aime jouer …	I like to play …
au ping-pong	ping pong
au tennis	tennis
au cricket	cricket
au hockey	hockey
aux échecs	chess
aux cartes	cards

Music

J'adore jouer …	I love to play …
du piano	the piano
du violon	the violin
de la guitare	the guitar
de la clarinette	the clarinet
J'aime écouter …	I like to listen to …
ma musique	my music
mon walkman	my Walkman
mes disques compacts / CD	my CDs
la radio	the radio

Reading

J'aime bien lire …	I really like reading …
les magazines / revues	magazines
les bandes dessinées / BD	comics
les romans	novels

TV / films

Je suis très content de regarder …	I'm very happy to watch …
la télévision	TV
les téléfilms	films made for TV
les films d'action	action films
les films d'aventure	adventure films
les films d'amour	romantic films
les comédies	comedies
les séries	series / serials
les feuilletons	soaps
les émissions de musique	music programmes
les émissions de nature	nature programmes

Quick Test

Read through this paragraph and answer the questions below:

Moi, j'aime bien lire, surtout les bandes dessinées et les romans historiques. De temps en temps je suis content de regarder les series et les feuilletons à la télé, mais je déteste les téléfilms! J'aime aussi la musique, le matin j'écoute la radio et après l'école j'adore jouer de la guitare avec mes copains.

1 Mention two things he reads.

2 What doesn't he like on TV?

3 What does he like to do after school?

4 What else suggests he likes music?

Extended vocabulary 1

Quand j'ai du temps libre …	When I've some free time …
Pendant mes heures de loisirs …	During my free time …

Places to go

au cirque	to the circus
au zoo	to the zoo
au jardin public	to the park
aux spectacles	to shows
aux pièces de théâtre	to plays
aux rencontres sportives	to sporting events
Ma passion, c'est faire …	What I really love is / are …
des promenades en bateau	boat outings
des balades en plein air	walks in the open air
des parties de tennis	games of tennis

Things you play

Je fais partie d'une équipe de rugby.	I play for a rugby team.
Je suis membre d'un club de judo.	I am a member of a judo club.

Ce que j'aime, c'est jouer …	What I like is playing …
d'un instrument	an instrument
du violoncelle	the cello
du clavier	the keyboard
de la batterie	the drums
de la flûte	the flute
de la flûte à bec	the recorder

More things to do

J'aime faire …	I like …
du bricolage	DIY / making things
du lèche-vitrines	window-shopping
de la peinture	painting
des jeux d'ordinateur	playing computer games

Quick Test

It's a good idea to write down one real example from TV next to each type of programme – try it!

Hobbies 2

Basic grammar

Using verbs

Look at some of the sentences you have covered in this section so far, noting in particular the verbs. Can you see any patterns?

Je **collectionne** des timbres.	I collect stamps.
Je **joue** aux échecs.	I play chess.
J'**écoute** mon walkman.	I listen to my Walkman.
Je **regarde** la télé.	I watch TV.

In French, verbs are either regular or irregular. Regular ones follow certain patterns. All the verbs shown here are regular and have infinitives ending in –er.
How does the *je* form end for –er verbs? In –e.

When learning verbs and phrases off by heart, try and spot the verb patterns as you go along: it will make remembering easier.

Irregular verbs, as you would expect, are a bit trickier. You need to learn the different forms for every verb.

je vais*	I go		je fais	I do
je sors	I go out		je lis	I read

*the infinitive = *aller*, but note this is an irregular verb

When two verbs are used together in the present tense, the second verb is in the infinitive.

J'**aime** aller au cinema.	I like to go the cinema.
J'**adore** écouter ma musique.	I love to listen to my music.
Je n'**aime** pas faire des promenades.	I don't like to go on walks.
Je **déteste** jouer au tennis.	I hate to play tennis.

For more information on verbs see **Tenses 1** pages 84–86.

Sport / games or music?

An important decision! In French, that's not the only thing you have to decide. Look at the examples, paying particular attention to the words in bold.

sports or games		*musical instruments*	
le football	Je joue **au** football.	**le** piano	Je joue **du** piano
la pétanque	Je joue **à la** pétanque.	**la** batterie	Je joue **de la** batterie.
l'ordinateur	Je joue **à l'**ordinateur.	**l'**orgue	Je joue **de l'**orgue.
les cartes	Je joue **aux** cartes.	**les** cymbals	Je joue **des** cymbales.

Extended vocabulary 2

Reading

J'adore lire …	I love to read …
les illustrés	illustrated magazines
les journaux	newspapers

les quotidiens	daily papers
romans policiers	detective novels
les magazines hebdomadaires	weekly magazines
les magazines mensuels	monthly magazines

Extended grammar

Using verbs to talk about what others do

All that we've covered in the **hobbies** chapter is about what *you* might do in *your* free time. But we all know that your teacher has been 'encouraging' you to use **variety**. So, what about writing about what **others** do?

		aller (to go)	*regarder* (to watch) and other –er verbs	*faire* (to do)	*lire* (to read)
I	*je*	*vais*	*regarde*	*fais*	*lis*
you	*tu*	*vas*	*regardes*	*fais*	*lis*
he she we	*il* *elle* *on*	*va*	*regarde*	*fait*	*lit*
we	*nous*	*allons*	*regardons*	*faisons*	*lisons*
you	*vous*	*allez*	*regardez*	*faites*	*lisez*
they they (f)	*ils* *elles*	*vont*	*regardent*	*font*	*lisent*

Quick Test *i*

Write four sentences using *je / il / on / ils* + the same verb.
Can you translate these sentences into English?

Quick Test **C**

Using the list of time phrases below for reference, can you try putting these into French:

- Every month
- Twice a week
- In the spring
- On Saturdays?

Time phrases

To make your writing and speaking more interesting, you will want to add some detail. The following time phrases are all useful:

normalement	*d'habitude*
genéralement	*tous les jours*
tous les samedis	*toutes les semaines*
le lundi	*le week-end*
le matin	*l'après midi*
le soir	*une fois par mois*
pendant l'été	*en hiver*
avant l'école	*après les cours*

No, there hasn't been some terrible mistake. **You** write in the English!

Top Tip
Be careful when using a dictionary, especially in exam conditions. It is really only intended for use in Reading and Writing assessments, although even in the Folio you should only use it to *check* the spelling or gender of key words (those you feel are needed for an answer). You are *not* allowed to use the dictionary in Listening assesments at all. So, there is an *extra* reason for committing as much vocabulary to memory as possible!

Extended vocabulary 3

TV/Films

Ce que je trouve passionnant, ce sont …	What I really find interesting is / are …
les films d'espionnage	spy films
les films de guerre	war films
les films de science-fiction	sci-fi films
les documentaires	documentaries

les actualités	the news
Ce que j'aime regarder, c'est …	What I like watching is / are …
la télé cablée	cable TV
la publicité	adverts
la météo	the weather forecast

Hobbies 3

Exercise 1

Read through this account of what Jean-Philippe does in his spare time.
Fill in the gaps with the correct form of the verb in brackets.

Tous les samedis je ____vais____ (aller) au parc avec mes copains.

Moi, je suis très sportif. Par exemple, tous les jours je _____ (faire) du

vélo avec mon père. Le soir, je _____ (aller) au club des jeunes ou on

_____ (jouer) au badminton ou au ping pong. Quelquefois, mon ami

Paul et moi, on _____ (faire) des promenades en bateau en été, s'il fait

beau. Autrement, j'_____ (aimer) aussi lire ou regarder la télévision.

Ma sœur, Aurélie, _____ (préférer) écouter ses disques compacts;

elle _____ (collectionner) des timbres aussi, ce que

je _____ (trouver) assez ennuyeux!

Exercise 2

Listen to this account of what Aurélie says about her weekends.
For each of her activities, choose the correct activity of the
two given.

1 *Généralement je lis beaucoup – en particulier les romans d'aventures / romans policiers.*

2 *De temps en temps, je fais du judo / karaté au centre sportif.*

3 *Le mercredi, on n'a pas de cours; alors je reste / rentre à la maison.*

4 *Je ne suis pas sportive, mais Françoise, ma copine, joue souvent au volley / basket pour l'équipe du collège.*

5 *Françoise et moi, on fait aussi pas mal de jeux vidéos / électroniques.*

Quick Test C

How many time phrases can you spot in **1–5** in exercise 2 above?

Extended vocabulary 4

Other			
chanter	to sing	*sortir le soir*	to go out in the evenings
danser	to dance	*monter à cheval*	to go horse-riding
dessiner	to draw	*bavarder avec **mes** copains*	to chat with my friends
collectionner des timbres	to collect stamps	***me** promener*	to go for walks
		***m'**amuser*	to have a good time

Exercise 3

4 Read through and listen to this questionnaire. Choose the answer closest to the truth for you!

Top Tip
Did you notice the use of the formal word for 'you' in French – *vous*? In the present tense, the *vous* form of regular verbs ends in –*ez*.

1 Est-ce que vous pratiquez du sport
   a souvent?
   b de temps en temps?
   c jamais ou presque jamais?

2 Jouez-vous
   a au tennis?
   b au foot?
   c au basket?

3 Faites-vous
   a du footing?
   b de la natation?
   c des promenades à pied?

4 Aimez-vous assister
   a aux matchs de football?
   b aux jeux Olympiques?
   c aux concours de danse?

5 À l'avenir, aimeriez-vous faire
   a de la planche à voile?
   b du ski nautique?
   c du ski de fond?

6 Votre célèbrité préférée est
   a comédien / comédienne de cinéma?
   b sportif / sportive qui joue pour son équipe nationale?
   c chanteur / chanteuse?

Now use your answers to write a paragraph in French, thinking carefully about how you would change the verbs (in particular).

Extended vocabulary 5

Expressing dislikes

J'ai horreur de …	I can't stand …	*Ce que je n'aime pas …*	What I don't like …
Je ne peux pas supporter …	I can't stand …	*Ça ne me dit rien de …*	What I don't like …
		Ce que déteste …	What I hate …

Education 1

Basic vocabulary

Subjects

À l'école, j'ai …	At school, I have…
je prends …	I take…
j'étudie …	I study…
l'allemand	German
l'anglais	English
la biologie /	biology
les sciences naturelles	
la chimie	chemistry
le commerce	commerce / business studies
le dessin	art / drawing
l'éducation physique et sportive (EPS)	PE
l'enseignement religieux	religious education
l'espagnol	Spanish
les études ménagères	home economics
le français	French
la géographie	geography
le grec	Greek CREDIT
la gymnastique	gymnastics
l'histoire	history
l'histoire-géo(graphie)	history / geography combined
l'informatique	computer studies
l'instruction civique	social education
l'italien	Italian
les langues modernes / étrangères	modern / foreign languages

le latin	Latin
les maths / les mathématiques	maths / mathematics
la musique	music
la philo / la philosophie	philosophy
la poterie	pottery
le russe	Russian
les sciences	science
le sport	sport / PE
la techno / la technologie	technology
les travaux manuels	CDT
les travaux pratiques	CDT

Forms

je suis en …	I'm in …
sixième …	P7
cinquième …	S1
quatrième …	S2
troisième …	S3
seconde …	S4
première …	S5
terminale …	S6

Look for patterns to help you remember: *le* for languages, *la* for sciences.

Extended vocabulary

Description of school

Je vais …	I go …
Il / elle va …	he / she goes …
à l'école primaire	to primary school
à l'école secondaire	to secondary school
au collège	to collège [French secondary school up to 16]
au lycée	to lycée [French secondary school 16–18]
mixte	(which is) mixed
pour les garçons	for boys
pour les filles	for girls
avec environ mille élèves	with about 1000 pupils
de 12 à 16 ans	from 12 to 16 (years)
qui se trouve …	which is situated …
à 10 kilomètres de Lyon	10 kilometres from Lyons
au centre-ville	in the town centre

en dehors du centre	outside the town centre
en banlieue	in the outskirts
en zone rurale	in the country *CREDIT*

Facilities / Equipment

Il y a ...	There is / are ...
Nous avons ...	We have ...
un centre de documentation	a resources centre
un foyer des élèves	a pupils' common room
un atelier de théâtre / danse	a theatre / dance studio

une bibliothèque	a library
une salle de professeurs	a staffroom
une salle polyvalente	a multi-purpose hall
une cour	a playground
une cantine	a canteen
une cafétéria de self-service	a self-service cafeteria
une piscine	a swimming pool
des salles de classe	(some) classrooms
des laboratoires	(some) laboratories
des vestiaires	(some) changing rooms
des ateliers de travaux pratiques	(some) CDT workshops
des courts de tennis	(some) tennis courts
des terrains de sport	(some) sports grounds / fields
beaucoup de magnétoscopes	lots of video machines
beaucoup de distributeurs de boissons	lots of drinks machines
beaucoup d'ordinateurs	lots of computers

Top Tip

Il faut and *il ne faut pas* are impersonal constructions – *il* doesn't refer to a person but to a thing: 'it is (not) allowed'.

Opinions about your school

POUR +

Il y a une bonne ambiance.	There's a good atmosphere.
Il y a des bons rapports entre élèves et profs.	There's a good relationship between pupils and teachers.
Les équipements sont bons.	The facilities are good.
Les locaux sont en bon état.	The buildings are in good condition.
Les salles de classes sont bien adaptées.	The classrooms are well equipped.
Nous avons beaucoup de clubs.	We have lots of clubs.
Nous avons des activités parascolaires.	We have after-school activities.

CONTRE –

La discipline n'est pas sérieuse.	Discipline isn't good.
Quelques élèves répondent aux profs.	Some pupils talk back to teachers.
Certains élèves causent des difficultés.	Certain pupils misbehave.
On n'aide pas les élèves en difficulté.	Weaker pupils don't get the support they need.
Il y a trop de contrôles.	There are too many assessments.

School rules

Il faut porter l'uniforme scolaire.	You have to wear school uniform.
On doit faire ses devoirs.	You have to do homework.
Il ne faut pas fumer.	You're not allowed to smoke.
On ne doit pas manger en classe.	You're not allowed to eat in class.

Quick Test

Using this last section on school rules, can you now draw up a list of dos and don'ts for your own school?

Education 2

Basic grammar

Daily routine at school

It is extremely useful to be able to describe your routine on a normal school day. For this, you will need to be 100 per cent about your present tense verbs and times in French:

Je me lève à sept heures.	I get up at 7 o'clock.	*À une heure moins le quart, on prend le déjeuner.*	At 12.45, we have lunch.
Je me lave.	I get washed.		
Je m'habille.	I get dressed.		
Je prends mon petit déjeuner.	I have breakfast.	*Moi, je mange à la cantine.*	I eat at the canteen.
du toast et des céréales	toast and cereal	*Les cours finissent à quatre heures moins vingt.*	School ends at 3.40.
Je quitte la maison vers huit heures et quart.	I leave the house at around 8.15.		
J'arrive au lycée à huit heures et demie.	I get to school at 8.30.	*Je rentre chez moi à quatre heures.*	I get home at 4.00.
Les cours commencent à neuf heures dix.	Lessons start at 9.10.	*Je fais mes devoirs.*	I do my homework.
		Ensuite nous mangeons.	After that we eat.
Les cours durent quarante minutes.	Lessons last 40 minutes.	*Puis je regarde un peu de télé …*	Then I watch a little TV …
Puis à dix heures et demie, c'est la récréation.	Break is at 10.30.	*et je me couche vers dix heures.*	and I go to bed at 10.00.

Reflexive verbs

Reflexive verbs have an extra word *after* the actual subject pronoun which means 'to myself' or 'to themselves' – in other words reflecting back on to the subject pronoun. You will find a lot of these verbs in the Daily Routine topic (the reflexive pronouns are shown in bold):

*je **me** réveille*	I wake up	*je **me** lève*	I get up	*je **me** lave*	I get washed
*je **m'**habille*	I get dressed	*je **me** douche*	I have a shower	*je **me** couche*	I go to bed

The actual reflexive pronoun, of course, changes according to the subject pronoun:

je me lave	*nous nous lavons*
tu te lave	*vous vous lavez*
il /elle / on se lave	*ils / elles se lavent*

Most verbs in French have an **–er** infinitive. A smaller number have an *–ir* or *–re* infinitive. These verbs have rules in the same way as the *–er* equivalents, and have different endings depending on who we are talking about:

–ir		**–re**	
finir (to finish)		**attendre** (to wait [for]; to expect)	
je finir	I finish	*j'attends*	I wait
tu finis	you finish	*tu attends*	you wait
il / elle / on finit	he / she /we finish	*il / elle / on attend*	he / she / we wait
nous finissons	we finish	*nous attendons*	we wait
vous finissez	you finish	*vous attendez*	you wait
ils / elles finissent	they finish	*ils / elles attendant*	they wait

(See **Tenses 1** on pages 84–86)

Extended grammar

CREDIT

Making decisions in your studies becomes increasingly important – what subjects to take, whether to stay on at school at all. To talk about this, you need to focus on expressing your intentions and then giving reasons for these.

Start with **what you intend to do**: note that the second part of the expression is in the infinitive.

je vais (I am going)	prendre (to take)	l'anglais
je veux (I want)	choisir (to choose)	les sciences nats
je compte (I intend)	étudier (to study)	l'histoire
j'ai l'intention de (I intend)	faire (to do)	la physique
j'espère (I hope)	laisser tomber (to drop)	le sport
		la philo

je voudrais (I would like)	quitter l'école (to leave school)
j'aimerais (I would like)	rester au lycée (to stay at school)

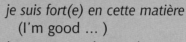

Top Tip
Folio markers are often looking for proof that you've tried to use a range of different ways of expressing yourself. The words *parce que* meaning 'because' are overused, so why not use some of the other phrases in the table below. Remember, *range* and *variety of expression* are key!

Then think about **why**: remember, you can use any of the connectives in the first box with any of the expressions in the second!

parce que (because)
puisque (since)
vu que (seeing as)
car (for)
à cause du fait que (on account of the fact that)

+ve
je suis fort(e) en cette matière
(I'm good …)
je trouve ce sujet passionnant
(it's really interesting)
ça serait très utile pour moi
(it would be very useful for me)
c'est facile (it's easy)

+ve
j'ai besoin de bonnes notes pour aller à la fac
(I need good grades to go to university)
je ne sais pas encore ce que je vais faire
(I still don't know what I'm going to do)
mes parents l'exigent
(my parents say I have to)

−ve
je suis nul(le) en … (I'm hopeless at …)
je la trouve ennuyeuse (it's really boring)
le prof n'explique jamais
(the teacher never explains)
c'est vraiment compliqué
(it's really complicated)

−ve
je déteste étudier (I hate studying)
j'ai déjà un boulot
(I've already got a job lined up)
je veux faire un apprentissage
(I want to do an apprenticeship)

Quick Test C

Put these into the most logical order!

a je m'habille
b je me couche vers onze heures du soir
c je me lève à sept heures
d je quitte la maison
e les cours finissent à quatre heures
f à dix heures et demie c'est la récré
g je fais mes devoirs
h je prends mon petit déjeuner

Quick Test i

Now consider your options for next year and write a ten-line account of your future intentions.

Education 3

Exercise 1

5

Thierry is in his last year at school – *terminale*. Listen to his account of two days of his timetable. Read through the timetable as you listen and answer the questions.

	lundi	mardi	mercredi	jeudi	vendredi	samedi
8h	maths	chimie		EPS	anglais	chimie
9h	maths	chimie		EPS	espagnol	chimie
10h	hist-géo	maths		biologie	espagnol	
récré						
10h40	philo	biologie		hist-géo	EPS	
11h40	permanence	musique		philo musique		
déjeuner						
13h30	anglais	informatique		maths	permanence	
14h30	anglais	informatique		maths	permanence	
15h30	biologie	anglais		informatique	philo	
16h30	biologie	permanence		dessin	philo	

*permanence = a study period

1 How many periods of PE does he have?
2 How many periods of IT does he have?
3 Which languages does he study?
4 Why do you think he is free on a Wednesday?
5 Which subject is surprisingly not on his timetable?
6 Mention any subject he has which you don't.
7 ... and vice versa!
8 Would you swap timetables with him? Why (not)?

Top Tip
When doing listening practice in preparation for your exam, remember to play the CD track three times and use each of the three playings in a certain way. You may decide just to listen the first time, then fill in different kinds of details the second and third times you listen.

Slang for school life

l'argot	slang
bosser / bucher	to swot
bachoter	to cram for an exam
potasser ses maths	to work hard at maths
le bahut	school
c'est barbant	it's boring
c'est pas la peine	it's not worth it

Quick Test C

Circle the odd one out on each line:

1 *lycée – école – collège – sœur*

2 *bibliothèque – cantine – récré – foyer*

3 *arriver – devoirs – rester – quitter*

4 *huit heures – professeur – trois heures et quart – quatre heures dix*

Exercise 2

6

Read through the text and listen at the same time to Sandrine and Lény discuss their plans for next year. Then decide whether the statements which follow each person's account are true or false.

> Moi, je crois que rester au lycée c'est une perte de temps. D'abord, même si je réussis à mes examens, je ne suis pas sûr d'avoir un emploi. Je connais pas mal de gens qui ont raté tous leurs examens qui n'ont jamais eu de bonnes notes à l'école, mais qui ont trouvé une très bonne situation. De l'autre côté, il y a ma sœur aînée qui, par exemple, a bien réussi à son bac et a fait son diplôme de commerce après, et qui n'a rien trouvé. Elle a vingt-deux ans et est toujours au chômage. Alors, à quoi ça sert de bosser? Étudier, c'est pas la peine! Moi, je vous le dis franchement, je vais quitter l'école dès que possible.

1 Sandrine has decided to stay on at school, in spite of her doubts. ☐

2 Some people she knows have got decent jobs without having passed exams. ☐

3 Her sister left school without her bac. ☐

4 Her sister is now unemployed. ☐

5 Sandrine is 22. ☐

> À mon avis l'éducation est vraiment importante pour l'avenir. Ceux qui ne font rien à l'école ont toujours du mal à trouver un bon emploi plus tard dans la vie. Ici en France on a besoin du bac non seulement pour trouver du travail mais pour aller à la faculté. Moi, personnellement, j'espère être reçu cette année, puis commencer mon bac littéraire. Peut-être qu'après j'irai en fac de droit. L'idée d'etre chômeur comme les élèves qui quittent le bahut sans diplôme me fait peur.

1 Lény thinks education is important for your future. ☐

2 He thinks it is unlikely that you can find a good job without working at school. ☐

3 He admits that anyone can get into university in France, even without the bac. ☐

4 He would like to go to study accountancy. ☐

5 He is scared of failing his exams. ☐

Quick Test ⓘ

Draw up two separate columns, headed **Agree** and **Disagree**. Write down comments from both texts above in the appropriate columns.

Top Tip

In Listening exercises it is worth remembering that you can write down the actual French words you hear if you can't quite get their English meaning right away. You'll have time at the end of the test to look over what you've written. But, do *not* give your final answers *in French* – this gets you zero marks!

Where I live 1

Basic vocabulary

Area

J'habite …	I live …
Nous habitons …	we live …
dans un appartement	in a flat
dans une petite / grande maison	in a small / big house
en ville	in town
au centre-ville	in the town centre
en banlieue	in the outskirts
en zone industrielle	in the industrial area
en zone rurale	in the country CREDIT
à la campagne	in the country
à cinq minutes de …	five minutes from …
dix kilomètres de …	ten kilometres from …
pas loin de …	not far from …
C'est une ville …	It's a … town.
pittoresque	picturesque
historique	historical
touristique	touristy
industrielle	industrial
de province	provincial

Top Tip
Notice the position of these longer adjectives – *after* the thing they describe.

avec trente mille habitants	with thirty thousand inhabitants
au centre …	in the centre …
au nord …	in the north …
au sud …	in the south …
à l'ouest	in the west …
à l'est	in the east …
de l'Écosse	of Scotland

Floors and rooms

Au sous-sol il y a …	In the basement there is …
un garage	a garage
une salle de jeux	a games room
une pièce de travaux / repassage	a utility room
Au rez-de-chaussée nous avons …	On the ground floor we have…
un salon / séjour	a living room
un bureau	a study
un W.C.	a toilet
une salle de séjour	a living room
une salle à manger	a dining room
une cuisine	a kitchen
une entrée	a hall
Au premier étage il y a …	On the first floor there is / are …
trois chambres	three bedrooms
une salle de bains	a bathroom
Au deuxième étage on a …	On the second floor we have …
le grenier	the attic

Bedroom

Ma chambre est …	My bedroom is …
assez / très …	quite / very …
petite / grande	small / big
jolie	nice
Il y a …	There is / are …
un lit	a bed
un ordinateur	a computer

un tapis	a carpet
une armoire	a wardrobe
une étagère	a bookshelf
une chaîne hi-fi / chaîne stéréo	a hi-fi
une télévision	a TV
des disques compacts / CD	(some) CDs
posters de …	(some) posters of …
mes affaires pour l'école	my things for school
C'est là où …	This is where …
je fais mes devoirs	I do my homework
je lis	I read
je me relaxe	I relax

Town places

Là où j'habite il y a …	Where I live there is / are …
un centre commercial	a shopping centre
un centre de loisirs	a leisure centre
un centre de sports	a sports centre
un château	a castle / stately home

un cinéma	a cinema
un commissariat	a police station
un hôpital	a hospital
un hôtel de ville	a town hall
un jardin public	a park
un marché	a market
un musée d'art / historique	a(n) art / history museum
un office du tourisme	a tourist information office
un parc	a park
un pont	a bridge
un stade	a sports stadium
un syndicat d'intiative	a tourist information office
un terrain de foot / rugby	a football / rugby pitch
un théâtre municipal	a public theatre
une alimentation générale	a general (food) store

une banque	a bank
une bibliothèque	a library
une boîte de nuit	a night club
une cathédrale	a cathedral
une disco	a disco
une église	a church
une gare (SNCF)	a train station
une gare routière	a bus station
une gendarmerie	a police station
la grande place	the main square
une poste	a post office
une station-service	a petrol station
une usine (de textiles)	a (textiles) factory

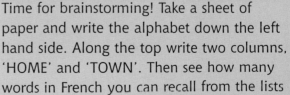

des boutiques	(some) boutiques / smart shops
des bistros	(some) bars
des brasseries	(some) bars that sell food
des bureaux (commerciaux)	(some) (business) offices
des cafés	(some) cafés
des grands immeubles	(some) blocks of flats
des grands magasins	(some) department stores
des hôtels	(some) hotels
des magasins	(some) shops
des monuments historiques	(some) historical monuments
des restaurants	(some) restaurants

Quick Test

Time for brainstorming! Take a sheet of paper and write the alphabet down the left hand side. Along the top write two columns, 'HOME' and 'TOWN'. Then see how many words in French you can recall from the lists above in three minutes. Like this:

	Home	Town
A	appartement	alimentation générale

Where I live 2

Top Tip
Remember to have variety in your French: use people or groups when introducing a topic (e.g. *Les touristes peuvent* …) and then use pronouns (e.g. *Ils peuvent* …).

Basic grammar

Use these phrases to start talking about where you live:

Il y a …	There is / are …
J'ai …	I have …
Nous avons …	We have …

To give more detail, you can use the verb *pouvoir* (to be able), plus an infinitive.

je peux	I can
tu peux	you can (singular informal, i.e. one person you know well)
il peut	he can
elle peut	she can
on peut	we / people can
nous pouvons	we can
vous pouvez	you can (singular formal / plural)
ils peuvent	they can (all male group or mixed group)
elle peuvent	they can (all female group)

Note in the following expressions how *pouvoir* is followed by an infinitive:

*On peut **aller** au parc / à la piscine.*	You can go to the park / swimming pool.
*Je peux **assister** aux matchs de rugby / à la fête régionale.*	I can go to rugby matches / the local festival.
*Ils peuvent **se balader** sur les collines / dans les montagnes.*	They can stroll in the hills / mountains.
*Tu peux **faire** des randonnées / du shopping.*	You can go for walks / shopping.
*Vous pouvez **vous promener** dans le jardin public / à la campagne.*	You can go for walks in the park / country.
*Elle peut **visiter** les monuments historiques / le château.*	She can visit the historical sights / the castle.
*Il peut **voir** l'église / la cathédrale.*	He can see the church / cathedral.

Remember to say what there *isn't* in your town or area: don't forget *un / une / des* become **de** after a negative.

*Il n'y a pas **de** cinéma.*	There isn't a cinema

Extended vocabulary 1

Home

Nous habitons …	We live in …
un grand immeuble	a big block of flats
un pavillon	a detached house
un studio	a small apartment / flat
une HLM	a council house / flat
un domicile de grand standing	an upmarket property
un domicile de luxe	a luxurious property

C'est un vieux bâtiment …	It's an old building …
en béton	made of concrete
en bois	made of wood
en brique	made of brick
en pierre	made of stone
qui est …	which is …
typique de la région	typical of the area
en bon / mauvais état	in good / bad condition

Extended grammar

Here are some interesting ways of saying what there is to do and see for *various groups* of people:

pour …	for …	*les sportifs*	sporty people
les habitants de …	the inhabitants of …	*les touristes*	tourists
les jeunes	young folk	*les étudiants*	students
les vieux	old folk	*les amateurs de …*	those who are keen on …

Other ways of doing this and of *adding variety* at the same time include:

Pour ceux qui s'intéressent à l'histoire …	For those who are interested in history …
Pour ceux qui sont passionnés de la culture …	For real culture vultures …
Si vous êtes à la recherche de la tranquilité …	If it's peace and quiet you're after …
Si vous voulez de la vie nocturne animée …	If you want lively night life …

Use these to lead into specific suggestions:

alors pourquoi pas essayer …	then why not try …
vous pourriez toujours visiter …	you could always visit …
vous devez prendre le bus à …	you should go by bus to …
la plage n'est pas loin …	the beach is not far …

Quick Test *i*

Prepare a poster for a new holiday resort, including many reasons for going there. Try to use a variety of expressions as well as a good choice of activities.

Quick Test *C*

Translate the following sentences into English:

1 *Vous pouvez vous promener dans le jardin public.*

2 *Je peux visiter les monuments historiques.*

3 *Les touristes peuvent faire du shopping au centre commercial.*

4 *Tu es sportif? Tu peux assister à un bon match de rugby.*

Extended vocabulary 2

Living room

Notre salle de séjour est	Our living room is …
très confortable	very comfy
Nous avons …	We have …
un grand canapé	a big sofa
un magnétoscope	a video recorder
une téléviseur	a television
une bibliothèque	a bookcase
une cheminée	a fireplace
une platine-laser	a CD player
une table basse	a coffee table
des fauteuils	(some) armchairs

des lampes	(some) lights
des tableaux aux murs	(some) paintings on the walls
On est très bien ici.	It's very cosy here.
C'est là où nous …	This is where we …
nous rejoignons le soir	gather in the evening
bavardons au sujet de la journée	talk about the day
causons	have a chat
discutons	talk
jouons du piano	play the piano
regardons la télé	watch TV

Where I live 3

Exercise 1

7

Listen to this description of someone's town and choose the correct word each time.

Nous habitons une petite / grande ville dans l'est / l'ouest de la France.

J'aime bien la région où j'habite parce qu'il y a beaucoup à faire et à voir / visiter ici.

Par exemple, vous pouvez faire des promenades à pied / cheval où bien aller vous promener dans le parc.

Deuxièmement, si vous êtes sportif / sympa, vous pourriez aller voir un match de foot / rugby le samedi matin / après-midi.

Nous avons pas mal de terrains de golf / sport dans notre ville.

Quand il fait beau, en été / automne, c'est vraiment très joli.

Même en hiver on peut faire / pratiquer du sport, car on fait du ski de fond / nautique.

Top Tip
When you come to write a piece on your home town, this can be done by simply replacing the options above with your own details. This can then be used as a model for a folio piece.

Exercise 2

CREDIT

8 Listen to and read through this interview with a grumpy old man about his home town of Gornac.

A Alors, Monsieur Grincheux, vous habitez où exactement?

B Comment?! Je ne vous entends pas! Répétez, jeune fille!

A Où habitez-vous, Monsieur Grincheux?

B Moi, j'habite à Gornac, un tout petit village dans le sud-ouest de la France.

A Gornac? Alors, je ne connais pas … ça se trouve où?

B Ah, mais vous ne savez pas grand-chose, vous! Eh bien, Gornac c'est à quelques kilomètres de Sauveterre …

A Sauveterre? Connais pas non plus! C'est dans quelle région?

B Bon, c'est à cent kilomètres environ de Bordeaux …

A Ah oui, je vois ou c'est … Et il y a combien d'habitants à … ?

B À Gornac!

A À Gornac?!

B Il y a … eh bien, vous savez, ça dépend de la saison, puisqu'en été on a quelques touristes, des Anglais, des Allemands … donc, je ne sais pas, moi, disons soixante-treize habitants.

A Comment? Soixante-treize habitants?! Et est-ce qu'il y a beaucoup de choses à faire et à voir à … ?

B À Gornac! Mais vous vous moquez de moi?! Écoutez, nous avons même une piscine en plein air maintenant, et en été, pendant les grandes vacances, les enfants se baignent dans la rivière juste à côté. C'est sympa.

GORNAC
Habitants
73
72

A Mais, Monsieur Grincheux, franchement …

B Quoi, franchement?!

A Avez-vous une discothèque à Gornac, une boîte de nuit, un centre de loisirs?

B Mais non, mais nous avons une petite maison de jeunes où on peut jouer aux échecs l'hiver ou même au badminton s'il fait beau …

A Alors, vous avez quand même quelques équipements sportifs à … ?

B À Gornac!! Mais bien sûr que oui. Et en plus, on peut passer des vacances actives ici … c'est bien pour les grands sportifs …

A Mais il ne faut pas exagérer, Monsieur Grincheux … des *vacances actives*! C'est ridicule! Vous n'avez pas assez d'habitants pour une équipe de foot …

B Alors là, jeune fille, vous vous trompez! L'année dernière nous avons gagné le Championnat des Quatres Fermes! Ah, les jeunes d'aujourd'hui!

Quick Test   C

Tick if it's in Gornac; cross if it's not.

	Yes	No
1 Football team	☐	☐
2 Multi-gym	☐	☐
3 Night club	☐	☐
4 Leisure centre	☐	☐
5 Disco	☐	☐
6 Play chess	☐	☐
7 Badminton	☐	☐

Make a list of reasons to visit Gornac.

Now pretend you are the interviewer and write an article in English trying to put people off the idea of spending their summer holidays in Gornac.

Quick Test   i

Make a list of phrases which suggest that Monsieur Grincheux is becoming irritable during the interview.

Extended vocabulary 3

Location

Nous habitons …	We live in …
une belle région	a nice area
un quartier …	a … area
agréable	pleasant
bruyant	noisy
cher / pas cher	dear / inexpensive
chic	smart
moche	grotty
snob	snooty
tranquille	quiet
Tout près il y a …	Nearby is / are …
un bois	a wood
un fleuve	a river

un lac	a lake
une forêt	a forest
une plage	a beach
une rivière	a river
des collines	(some) hills
des montagnes	(some) mountains
Nous avons beaucoup …	We have lots …
de circulation	of traffic
de monde	of people
de touristes	of tourists
de voitures	of cars
d'endroits pour les enfants	of children's areas
d'espaces verts	of green areas

Transport 1

Basic vocabulary

Types of transport

Je prends …	I take …
l'autobus	the bus
l'avion	the plane
le bateau	the boat
le camion	the lorry
le car	the coach
le car-ferry	the car ferry
le ferry	the ferry
le hovercraft / l'aéroglisseur (m)	the hovercraft
le métro	the underground
le train	the train
le TGV	the TGV [French high-speed train]
le tramway	the tram
le vélo	the bike
la moto	the motorbike
la motocyclette	the moped
la voiture	the car

Bus / underground

un arrêt d'autobus / de métro	a bus / underground stop

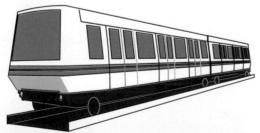

un carnet	a booklet of tickets
composter	to stamp / validate your ticket
un composteur	a ticket stamping machine
correspondance	connection
une gare routière	a bus station
numéro	(bus) number / line
un passage souterrain	underground passage / walkway
une station de métro	underground station
tarif	cost of ticket
un ticket	ticket

Ferry

une gare maritime	ferry terminal
une traversée	a crossing
sortie de secours	emergency exit
le tunnel sous la Manche	Channel Tunnel

Train

un aller-simple	a single ticket
un aller-retour	a return ticket
arrivées	arrivals
un billet	a ticket
un buffet	a buffet
le chemin de fer	railway

une consigne automatique	a left-luggage locker
départs	departures
entrée	entrance
fumeurs / non-fumeurs	smoking / non-smoking
une gare SNCF	a train station
un guichet	a ticket office
un horaire	a timetable
journaux	newspapers
un quai	a platform
renseignements	information
réservations	reservations
un retard	a delay
une salle d'attente	a waiting room
sortie	exit
un tarif supplémentaire	an additional charge
une voie	a track
voyageurs	travellers

Plane

un aéroport	an airport
atterrissage	landing
un avion	an aeroplane
une ceinture de sécurité	safety belt
décollage	take-off
la douane	customs
une hôtesse de l'air	an air hostess
un passeport	a passport
un pilote	a pilot
rien à déclarer	nothing to declare
un steward	an air steward
un vol	a flight

Car

l'arrière	rear (of car)
l'avant	front (of car)
la clé / clef	key
le coffre	boot
les essuies-glace	window-wipers
les freins	brakes
le moteur	engine
le pare-brise	windscreen
les phares	headlights
le pneu	tyre
le rétroviseur	driving mirror
le siège	seat
en retard	late

Extended vocabulary 1

Bus

Où est l'arrêt d'autobus?	Where is the bus stop?
Il y a un bus tous les combien?	How often does the bus come?
À quelle heure part le prochain / dernier bus?	When is the next / last bus?
C'est bien l'autobus pour le centre-ville?	Is this the right bus for the town centre?
Vous descendez à l'hôtel de ville.	You get off at the town hall.

Underground

Pour … c'est quelle direction, s'il vous plaît?	What line is it for … ?

Train

Je voudrais un billet pour Paris.	I would like a ticket for Paris.
première / deuxième classe	first / second class
Je voudrais réserver une place non-fumeur.	I would like to book a seat in non-smoking.
Le train de Lyon arrive à quelle heure?	When does the train from Lyons arrive?
Sur quel quai?	On what platform?
Le train pour Avignon part à quelle heure?	When does the train for Avignon leave?

De quel quai?	From which platform?
C'est direct ou faut-il changer?	Is it direct or do you have to change?
le train en provenance de Nîmes	the train from Nîmes
le train en destination de Rennes	the train for Rennes
deux minutes d'arrêt	stopping for two minutes

Quick Test C

Find the French for:
1 ticket stamping machine
2 walkway
3 booklet of tickets
4 left luggage locker
5 timetable

Quick Test i

Write a brief dialogue featuring a tourist at a train station, including the most difficult language. Find a picture of a train or travel scene and stick your dialogue to the picture. This will help you to envisage scenes when doing listening exercises.

Transport 2

Basic grammar

When describing travel you do routinely, you need to use the *present tense*.

The main verbs you use are *prendre* (to take) and *aller* (to go).

Remember to make your French more interesting by including time phrases.

tous les ans	every year	*ensuite*	next
chaque année	every year	*puis*	then
en été	in the summer	*et après ça*	and after that
je prends	I take	*je vais*	I go
on prend	we take	*on va*	we go
nous prenons	we take	*nous allons*	we go
l'avion	the plane	*par le train*	by train
le train	the train	*en car*	by coach
la voiture	the car	*en autobus*	by bus
de Newcastle à Paris	from Newcastle to Paris	*à Poitiers*	to Poitiers
		en France	in France

Extended vocabulary 2

Plane

Je voudrais un billet …	I would like a(n) … ticket.
classe touriste	tourist class
classe économique	economy class
Est-ce qu'il y a un vol pour Londres … ?	Is there a flight to London … ?
ce matin	this morning
cet après-midi	this afternoon
ce soir	this evening
aujourd'hui	today
demain	tomorrow
Le vol dure combien de temps?	How long is the flight?

Je cherche un chariot.	I'm looking for a trolley.
J'ai perdu ma valise.	I've lost my suitcase.
J'ai quelque chose à declarer.	I've got something to declare.
Où se trouve la station de taxis?	Where is the taxi rank?
Est-ce qu'il y a un car qui va au centre-ville?	Is there a coach to the town centre?

Driving

toutes directions	all main routes
autres directions	other directions
autoroute	motorway
péage	toll
priorité à droite / gauche	give way (to vehicles from right / left)
vous avez la priorité	you have right of way
un rond-point	a roundabout
les feux	traffic lights
une station-service	a petrol station
sans plomb	lead free
gazole	diesel
la pression des pneus	tyre pressure
Zut! Je suis tombé en panne!	Blast! I've broken down!

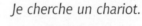

CREDIT

Extended grammar

When describing travel in the past, use the perfect tense or (*passé composé*) for events and single completed actions. See **Tenses 3** on pages 90–93.

l'année dernière	last year
l'été dernier	last summer
pendant les grandes vacances	during the summer holidays
j'ai pris	I took
on a pris	we took
nous avons pris	we took
le car-ferry	the car ferry
le bateau	the boat
le hovercraft	the hovercraft
de Douvres à Calais	from Dover to Calais
et le lendemain	and the next day
je suis allé(e)	I went
on est allé(e)s	we went
nous sommes allé(e)s	we went
en voiture	by car
au camping dans le sud de la France	to the campsite in the south of France

Top Tip
When the perfect tense is formed with *être*, you need to add an **-e** to the participle when the subject is feminine – *elle est allée*.

To describe something in the past – such as how the journey was – you use the imperfect tense. See **Tenses 3** on pages 90–93.

*Le voyage **était** …*	The journey was …
long	long
ennuyeux	boring
inconfortable	uncomfortable

CARTE POSTALE

Salut les copains!

Nous voici à Londres! Vendredi on a pris le ferry de Douvres à Calais – le voyage n'était pas long. Samedi, nous sommes allés en voiture à Salisbury, c'était magnifique. Ensuite, Gérard est parti avec son corres, William, au camping.

Tout va bien!

Grosses bises,

Patricia xxx

Quick Test

Write a postcard to your friend at home, telling her of the disastrously long and complicated journey you have endured to get to your destination.

Quick Test

Read the postcard then answer the following questions:

1 How did they travel to England?

2 Where are they now?

3 How did they get to Salisbury?

4 Who has Gérard gone camping with?

Transport 3

Exercise 1

Label as many things as you can in this picture of a train station.

Exercise 2

Unjumble these French transport words, then translate them into English.

Anagrams	French	English
postercom		
rage tièruoe		
ioncam		
airehor		
Lasel d'enattte		
geursvoya		
olv		
rifta lésuppmentaire		
pondancecorres		

Top Tip
Solving anagrams is a sure way of helping you remember some of the most difficult words. You and a friend could try making some up for each other, or you could ask a parent to make up a few for you.

Exercise 3

9

Listen to these travel announcements. Try to get down as much detail as you can about each one after three listenings. Try listening to the CD with the book closed. Once you've written your answers open the book again and check them against the following transcript:

1   Le train en provenance de Nîmes arrivera au quai numéro cinq dans dix minutes.

2   Le vol Air France 307 en destination de Londres aura une heure de retard.

3   Le prochain train pour Paris partira du quai numéro 12b à 21h 35.

4   Le buffet fermera à 23 heures ce soir.

5   Attention, passagers du TGV de Nice: ce train n'aura pas d'arrêt. *CREDIT*

6   Attention, attention: un passeport britannique vient d'être présenté aux objets trouvés.

7   À cause du mauvais temps et du brouillard le vol en destination de Moscou aura deux jours de retard. Tous les passagers sont priés de se présenter au bureau Air Flot immédiatement!

Quick Test   C

Test yourself – past or present? Decide for each one.

1 on prend _____   **2** nous avons pris _____   **3** je suis allée_____

4 l'année dernière _____   **5** cet été _____   **6** on va _____

7 on est allé _____

Holidays 1

Basic vocabulary

General

Types of holiday

un échange scolaire	a school exchange
la fête	festival
les grandes vacances	summer holidays
les jours de congé	days off
un séjour	a stay / visit
les vacances d'été	summer holiday
les vacances d'hiver	winter holiday
les vacances de Noël	Christmas holidays
les vacances de neige / ski	skiing holiday
les vacances de Pâques	Easter holidays
une visite scolaire	a school visit / trip
le voyage	journey

Types of accommodation

une auberge de jeunesse	youth hostel
un camping	campsite
la chambre d'hôte	Bed and Breakfast; guest room
un gîte	self-catering
un hôtel	hotel
une pension	guest house

Locations

au bord de la mer	at the seaside
au bord de la rivière	by the river
à la campagne	in the countryside
à la montagne	in the mountains
à l'étranger	abroad

Destinations

à Édimbourg en Écosse	in Edinburgh in Scotland
à Madrid en Espagne	in Madrid in Spain
à Paris en France	in Paris in France
à Rome en Italie	in Rome in Italy
à Montréal au Canada	in Montreal in Canada
à Lisbon au Portugal	in Lisbon in Portugal
à Disney World aux États-Unis	at Disney World in the USA

Hotel

l'ascenseur	lift
une chambre avec …	a room with…
bain	a bath
balcon	a balcony
douche	a shower
télévision	a TV
WC	a toilet
une chambre à deux personnes	a double room
la clé / clef	key
la demi-pension	half-board
pension complète	full-board
au rez-de-chaussée	on the ground floor
au premier étage	on the first floor
au deuxième étage	on the second floor
un hotel de luxe / grand confort	a luxury hotel
ouvert toute l'année	open all year round
fermé le mois de janvier	closed for the month of January
payer les arrhes	to pay a deposit
Le petit déjeuner est compris / non-compris.	Breakfast is included / not included.
non-compris	not included
le prix	price
le tarif	price list
la réception	reception
le réceptionniste	receptionist
la sortie de secours	emergency exit

Camping

le bloc sanitaire	wash and toilets area
le bureau d'accueil	reception / check-in
la camping	campsite
l'électricité	electricity
l'eau non-potable	non-drinking water
les emplacements de tente	sites for tents

Top Tip

à is used for a town or city and can mean either 'to' or 'in'
en, au, aux are used for countries and can mean either 'to' or 'in'
la France → en France;
le Canada → au Canada;
les États-Unis → aux Etats-Unis

caravanes	caravans	**Youth hostel**	
grandes caravanes	mobile homes	*l'auberge de jeunesse*	youth hostel
la laverie	laundry	*la carte d'adhérent*	membership card
la lessive	clothes washing	*les couvertures*	blankets
les machines à laver	washing machines	*le dortoir des filles*	girls' dormitory
les poubelles	rubbish bins	*le dortoir des garçons*	boys' dormitory
les prises de courant	electrical sockets *CREDIT*	*les draps*	sheets
la salle de jeux	games room	*la mère / le père*	female / male warden
les bouteilles de gaz	gas containers	*aubergiste*	
les bouteilles de glace	bottles containing ice		
les lampes électriques	electric lamps		
les sacs de couchage	sleeping bags		
les canifs	penknives		
les allumettes	matches		
les bols	bowls		
la cuisinière de gaz	gas cookers		

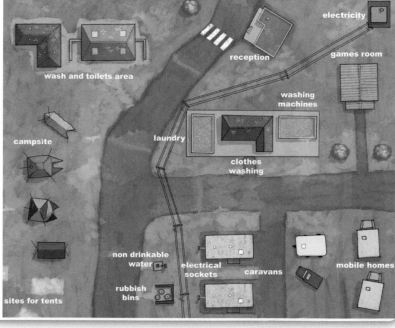

Extended vocabulary

General accommodation phrases

Je voudrais réserver …	I would like to reserve …
une chambre à deux lits	a room with twin beds
pour cinq nuits	for five nights
du quinze au vingt août	from 15 to 20 August
C'est à quel nom, s'il vous plaît?	In which name, please?
Vous avez de la place pour une tente?	Do you have a space for a tent?
C'est pour combien de personnes?	For how many people?
Quels sont les tarifs, s'il vous plaît?	What are the prices, please?
Le petit déjeuner est compris?	Is breakfast included?
Voulez-vous remplir cette fiche?	Would you like to fill in this form?

Y a-t-il un parking?	Is there a car park?
Le parking est juste à coté / derrière.	The car park is just next door / behind.
Il y a un problème avec le téléviseur.	There's a problem with the TV.
La douche ne marche pas.	The shower's broken.
L'ascenseur est en panne.	The lift is out of order.

Quick Test

Draw your ideal hotel room, labelling as many of its features and facilities as you can in French. Then try memorising them. See how many you can recall in a minute. Stick this up on your bedroom door at home.

Holidays 2

Basic grammar

An important aspect of the **Holidays** topic is understanding rules and regulations, dos and don'ts, what is and what isn't allowed. *Devoir* is a very useful verb in this context.

Must / should

Use *devoir* in the present tense to talk about what you *must* do:

je dois	I must	*nous devons*	we must
tu dois	you must	*vous devez*	you must
il / elle doit	he / she must	*ils / elles doivent*	they must
on doit	we / people must		

Use *devoir* in the conditional to talk about what you *should* do (see **Tenses 2** on pages 87–89):

je devrais	I should	*nous devrions*	we should
tu devrais	you should	*vous devriez*	you should
il / elle devrait	he / she should	*ils / elles devraient*	they should
on devrait	we / people should		

CREDIT

In both cases, *devoir* is usually followed by a second verb in the infinitive.

… **faire** une réservation	… make a booking
… **payer** les arrhes	… put down a deposit
… **laisser** la clé à la réception	… leave your key at reception
… **ranger** les dortoirs	… tidy the dorms
… **rentrer** avant 22 heures	… get back before 10.00 p.m.

il faut ('it is necessary to / you need to') is an alternative to *devoir*. It is also followed by a verb in the infinitive.

*Il faut **faire** son lit le matin.*   You have to make your bed in the morning.

Must not / should not

When talking about what is not allowed, there are a few possibilities.

1   Use **ne … pas** with *devoir* or *il faut*. Remember it goes around the verb.

*Tu **ne** dois **pas** rentrer trop tard.*	You must not come back too late.
*Vous **ne** devriez **pas** manger dans les chambres.*	You should not eat in your rooms.
*Il **ne** faut **pas** jouer de la musique après 21 heures.*	You must not play music after 9 p.m.

2   Use these phrases:

Il est défendu de fumer dans l'ascenseur.
   It is forbidden to smoke in the lift.
Il est interdit de manger dans le séjour.
   It is forbidden to eat in the lounge.
Sometimes you see signs with simply 'no … -ing', e.g.
DÉFENSE DE FUMER   NO SMOKING

Top Tip

Défense de fumer is typical exam vocabulary, particularly to do with what is not allowed in public places, such as hotels, parks, etc. Note how the infinitive of the verb is used here! This makes it easy to use a dictionary!

Extended grammar

To talk about a holiday in the past, you need the perfect tense (*passé composé*)
see **Tenses 3** on pages 90–93. Most verbs form the perfect tense with **avoir**.

j'**ai**		I	
on **a**	**logé** *dans un hôtel*	we	stayed in a hotel
nous **avons**		we	

j'**ai**		I	
on **a**	**fait** *du camping*	we	went camping
nous **avons**		we	

j'**ai**		I	
on **a**	**passé** *deux nuits à l'hôtel*	we	spent two nights in the hotel
nous **avons**		we	

Some verbs use **être** (you need to learn which do – there aren't many):

je **suis resté(e)**		I	
on **est resté(e)s**	*dans une pension*	we	stayed in a guest house
nous **sommes resté(e)s**		we	

Finally, don't forget to give an opinion on your holiday
accommodation! For this, you'll remember, you have to
use the imperfect tense.

Le camping **était** …	The campsite was …
formidable!	brilliant!
bien aménagé	well looked after

But when you got to the youth hostel, the warden was
not so great!

Le père aubergiste était …	The warden was …
trop sévère!	too strict!
casse-pieds!	a pain!

Top Tip

Compare the past participles of *avoir* and *être* verbs. In *avoir* verbs, the participle doesn't change, but in *être* verbs, it adds **–e** and or **–s** when the subject is feminine / plural.

Quick Test

Make up your own (amusing) list of forbidden things in the
campsite, using *DÉFENSE DE* … followed by a verb in the infinitive.

e.g. *DÉFENSE DE MANGER LES CHIENS DANS LE PARKING*

Quick Test

Translate the following sentences into English:

1 *Vous devriez laisser la clef à la reception.*

2 *On devrait rentrer avant 22 heures.*

3 *Les clients devraient payer les arrhes immédiatement.*

4 *Les garçons devraient ranger les dortoirs tous les matins.*

Holidays 3

Exercise 1

Use the sentences to write a dialogue between the tourist and hotel manager.
(You will have to put the sentences in the correct order.) You may also wish to
add a phrase or two!

Tourist

- Mais j'ai réservé la chambre il y a un mois!
- La douche ne fonctionne pas!
- Le petit déjeuner est compris?
- Je m'appelle Henri Martin. J'ai fait une réservation pour deux chambres.
- L'ascenseur est en panne?
- La chambre est trop bruyante – elle donne directement sur la rue principale!
- C'est à quel étage, s'il vous plaît?
- Où se trouve la chambre?

Hotel manager

- Je regrette, monsieur, c'est la seule chambre disponible!
- Bonjour, monsieur. Que puis-je faire pour vous?
- Je ne trouve pas de réservation à ce nom …
- Ah non, monsieur, je regrette encore, mais le petit déjeuner est
  supplémentaire.
- Oui, monsieur. Prenez l'escalier!
- Votre chambre est au troisième étage.
- Nous avons une chambre libre …
- Je vais téléphoner immédiatement au plombier.

Exercise 2

Madame Laguerre, an elderly and extremely strict female warden of the youth hostel at Belgrange in the south of France, 'welcomes' a group of school children on their first visit there …

10

'Et bien, bonsoir, les enfants. Permettez-moi de me présenter: je suis votre mère aubergiste ici à l'auberge de jeunesse de Belgrange. Tout d'abord, je voudrais vous parler de nos règlements, car il y en a BEAUCOUP, vous savez!

Premièrement, les garçons, vous n'avez PAS LE DROIT de monter au troisième étage, car le troisième étage est réservé aux filles. Donc, pour vous il est FORMELLEMENT INTERDIT d'y aller. Espérons que c'est bien clair!

CREDIT

Deuxièmement, il est ABSOLUMENT DÉFENDU de fumer dans l'auberge.

Les fumeurs seront immédiatement renvoyés de mon établissement! D'ailleurs, j'ai horreur des cigarettes!

Autre chose … il ne faut PAS JOUER AU FOOTBALL dans les dortoirs. Vous n'êtes pas dans une colonie de vacances ici. Franchement, on n'est pas là pour s'amuser! Il y a un terrain de sport à cent metres d'ici, alors je vous prie de jouer dehors!

Les visiteurs n'ont PAS LE DROIT de manger dans le vestibule, ni dans la salle de séjour non plus. Vous serez servis dans la salle à manger, comme il est normal! On n'est pas dans un camping ici, je vous le dis!

Pour en finir, il faut que je vous le dise, il est STRICTEMENT INTERDIT de chanter – soit dans les toilettes, soit dans les douches, après 21 heures.

Bon, c'est fini pour aujourd'hui, les garçons et les filles. Alors amusez-vous bien … mais … surtout ne faites pas trop de bruit dans les couloirs!'

Quick Test ⓘ

Copy out the 'don't' signs onto postcard-size cardboard and pin them up around the house (having first secured permission, of course!).

Top Tip
Remember that you have to look up the infinitive of the verb and then take that meaning back to the actual tense and subject in the passage, in order to get the full meaning in the text.

Make a list of all the things which the children are forbidden to do!

Top Tip
The key words in a passage are often nouns or verbs. Look over the above text, and see how you get on with looking up the meaning of the following words in your dictionary – this should greatly increase your understanding of the passage!

nouns	verbs
mère aubergiste	parler
règlement	monter
garçon	fumer
fumeurs	être renvoyé
établissement	(renvoyer)
vestibule	s'amuser
couloir	chanter
douche	

Eating out 1

Basic vocabulary – drinks and snacks

Cold drinks

boissons froides	cold drinks
cidre	cider
citron pressé	squeezed fresh lemon juice
coca	coke
crème de menthe	mint drink [bright green!]
eau minérale	mineral water
gazeuse / non-gazeuse	sparkling / still
eau plate	still water
fanta	Fanta
grenadine	grenadine [pomegranate-flavoured red drink]
jus de fruits	fruit juice
jus de pomme	apple juice
jus de pamplemousse	grapefruit juice
jus de tomates	tomato juice
jus d'ananas	pineapple juice
jus d'orange	orange juice
limonade	lemonade
orangina	Orangina [fizzy orange drink]

Hot drinks

boissons chaudes	hot drinks
café	coffee
café-crème	coffee with cream
café au lait	coffee with milk
chocolat (chaud)	hot chocolate
express	espresso
thé	tea
thé citron	lemon tea
thé au lait	tea with milk

Alcoholic drinks

boissons alcoolisées	alcoholic drinks
apéritif	aperitif [pre-dinner drink]
bière allemande	German beer
bière anglaise	English beer
bière blonde	lager / light beer
bière brune	brown beer
bière pression	draught beer
panaché	shandy
vin de table	table wine [ordinary]
vin blanc	white wine
vin rosé	rosé wine
vin rouge	red wine

Snacks

casse-croûte	snacks
crêpes	pancakes
crêpe citron	pancake with lemon
crêpe confiture	pancake with jam
croque-monsieur	toasted cheese and ham sandwich
glace	ice-cream
quiche lorraine	egg and ham quiche
pizza	pizza
sandwich au fromage	cheese sandwich
sandwich au jambon	ham sandwich

Top Tip

When you see the sign CONSOMMATIONS, this will give the prices for drinking and eating at the bar only – the prices if you are sitting down will be higher! You have been warned!

Extended vocabulary – restaurant

MENU À 20 EUROS	20 EURO MENU
HORS D'ŒUVRE	STARTERS
assiette de crudités	plate of raw cut vegetables
escargots	snails
moules marinières	mussels in white wine
pâté de foie gras	liver paté
consommé	clear soup
soupe à l'oignon (à partir de 20 heures)	onion soup (evening only)
potage du jour	soup of the day
PLATS CHAUDS / PRINCIPAUX	MAIN DISHES
plat du jour	dish of the day
omelette aux champignons	mushroom omelette
poulet rôti	roast chicken
escalope de veau	veal escalope
canard à l'orange	duck in orange sauce
steak grillé	grilled steak
bœuf bourgignon	beef stew / casserole
gigot d'agneau	leg of lamb
choucroute	sauerkraut [cabbage in vinegar]
truite aux amandes	trout in almonds
fruits de mer	shellfish
huîtres	oysters
salade de tomates	tomato salad
salade composée	mixed salad

VEGETABLES	
légumes au choix	choice of vegetables
haricots verts	green beans
champignons	mushrooms
carottes	carrots
petits pois	peas
pommes de terre	potatoes
riz	rice
frites	chips
CHEESES	
fromages	cheeseboard
brie normande	brie from Normandy
camembert	camembert
chèvre	goat's cheese
DESSERTS	
desserts	sweets
fruits de la saison	fruit of the season
melon	melon
pastèque	water melon
yaourt	yoghurt
crème brûlée	crème brulée
crème caramel	crème caramel
tarte aux pommes	apple tart
gâteau au chocolat	chocolate cake
glace	ice-cream
à la fraise	strawberry
à la framboise	raspberry
à la vanille	vanilla
Service non compris	service not included
TVA compris	VAT included

Quick Test C

Place these foods under the correct category:

Starter	Main course	Veg	Cheese	Dessert

Quick Test i

Design a lunchtime menu for a local seaside restaurant which specialises in seafood and fresh produce.

1 *Chèvre*
2 *Épinards*
3 *Tarte aux pommes*
4 *Pâté de foie gras*
5 *Poulet rôti*
6 *Canard à l'orange*
7 *Pastèque*
8 *Pommes de terre*
9 *Haricots verts*
10 *Glace à la framboise*

Eating out 3

Exercise 1

Work out these French anagrams of food and drink items.

Next learn the French words.

Finally, try translating them into English.

Anagrams	French	English
DRINKS		
inv		
ginaoran		
tronci sspreé		
pressex		
latchooc		
SNACKS		
crpêe		
wichsand ua agefrom		
cglae		
zazpi		
quecro-sieurmon		
pichs		

Exercise 2

 Imagine you are a tourist.
Read and listen to what the waiter says and respond appropriately.

1 Bonjour! C'est pour combien de personnes, s'il vous plaît?

2 Vous voulez voir quel menu?

3 Alors, vous avez choisi?

4 Et comme boisson?

5 Vous le voulez comment, votre steak?

6 Vous voulez commander un dessert?

7 Vous venez d'où en Écosse?

8 Bonne journée, Messieurs-dames!

Top Tip
You should have noticed by now how the custom is to use the word *vous* instead of *tu* in a café and restaurant context. This is because the situation is formal – those involved don't know each other.

Exercise 3

12 Listen to these five orders without looking at the text below. Once you have written your answers refer to the text below to check them.
Give details of the order and the total bill for each table.

1 Alors, table cinq: un gigot d'agneau et un poulet rôti. Onze euros cinquante.

2 Table numéro douze. On a commandé deux express et une glace à la vanille. Ça fait trois euros dix.

3 L'addition pour table six: deux fois moules marinières et une pizza. À boire, une carafe de vin blanc.

4 La table quinze: un steak-frites, une salade composée, un potage du jour et une choucroute … deux bières, une eau minérale et un coca. Vingt-trois euros soixante-dix.

5 Les Anglais à la table quatre: demi-douzaine d'escargots, une escalope de veau, une bouteille de vin rouge. Ça fait treize … plus trois cinquante, alors, seize euros cinquante en tout, voilà!

Top Tip
How to make plurals in French is mostly straight forward – you simply add an –*s* as we do in English. The only problem here is that you won't hear the –*s*!
In some cases, the word ending is changed slightly, e.g. *le journal* (newspaper) becomes *les journaux*.

Quick Test

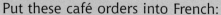

Put these café orders into French:

2 white coffees	3 lemon teas
1 pineapple juice	1 coffee with cream
3 ham sandwiches	2 vanilla ice-creams
1 toasted sandwich	1 pâté sandwich
1 pancake with jam	2 cokes
1 pancake with lemon	1 fizzy water

Relationships 1

Basic vocabulary

Top Tip

Feminine agreement has been shown after the masculine version of adjectives: in brackets where a letter is added, e.g. *charmant(e)*, or after an oblique where the ending is replaced, e.g. *généreux / euse*. This is to highlight how the feminine is formed and to help you revise the different ways.

aimable	nice
agréable	pleasant
amusant(e)	funny
artistique	artistic
bavard(e)	chatty
calme	calm
charmant(e)	charming
compréhensif / ve	understanding
doux / ce	mild
drôle	funny
dynamique	dynamic
équilibré(e)	well balanced
extraverti(e)	extrovert
formidable	great
généreux / euse	generous
honnête	decent, honest
indépendant(e)	independent
intelligent(e)	intelligent
loyal(e)	loyal
modeste	modest, simple
mûr(e)	mature
obéissant(e)	obedient

ordonné(e)	tidy
ouvert(e)	open
paisible	peaceful, quiet
patient(e)	patient
poli(e)	polite
raisonnable	reasonable
respectueux / euse	respectful
rigolo(te)	funny, a laugh
sage	well behaved
sensible	sensitive
sérieux / euse	serious
sociable	sociable
sympa or *sympathique*	nice
tendre	gentle
tranquil(le)	calm, quiet
travailleur / euse	hardworking

Top Tip

Remember to use negative constructions with *ne … pas* to extend the range of what you can say e.g. *Il est intelligent, mais il n'est pas agréable!* (He's intelligent, but not pleasant!) or *On a beaucoup en commun, mais on ne s'entend pas bien!* (We've lots in common, but we don't get on!). Note the position of the particles *ne* and *pas*!

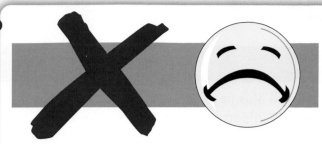

agité(e)	worked up, uptight
aggressif / ve	aggressive
antipathique	dislikeable
arrogant(e)	arrogant
autoritaire	authoritarian
bête	stupide
bruyant(e)	noisy
casse-pieds	annoying, a pain
désagréable	unpleasant

désobéissant(e)	disobedient
désordonné(e)	untidy
égoïste	selfish
embêtant(e)	annoying
ennuyeux / euse	boring
fâché(e)	angry
idiot(e)	stupid
impatient(e)	impatient
inquiet / ète	worried
insolent(e)	insolent
jaloux / ouse	jealous
malhonnête	dishonest
méchant(e)	horrible
paresseux / euse	lazy
sévère	strict
violent(e)	violent

Extended vocabulary

How we are together

On s'entend bien.	We get on well.
On discute.	We discuss things.
On ne se dispute pas beaucoup.	We don't argue much.
On fait tout ensemble.	We do everything together.
On a beaucoup de choses en commun.	We have lots of things in common.
On rigole.	We have a good time.
On s'amuse.	We enjoy ourselves.
On sort ensemble.	We go out together.
On se dispute.	We don't get on.
On ne s'entend pas bien.	We don't get on well.
On s'entend mal.	We get on badly.
On ne discute pas.	We don't discuss things.

Quick Test

Say what is positive and negative each time about these family members:

1 ma mère est travailleuse, mais pas toujours raisonnable

2 mon petit frère est mûr pour son âge mais trop bavard

3 ma sœur aînée est artistique, mais égoïste

4 il est rigolo, mon père, mais parfois trop bruyant

Quick Test

Write out the phrases which best describe your own relationship with a member of your family.

Relationships 2

Basic grammar

To give a more detailed account of a relationship, you will also need to be able to describe what people do. In this context, it is obviously important to be able to use a range of verbs accurately. Let's take as an example a (male) friend you get on really well with. Note the use of *il* all the way through.

Il me comprend.	He understands me.
Il m'encourage avec …	He encourages me with …
Il me respecte.	He respects me.
Il me fait confiance.	He trusts me.
Il s'entend bien avec moi.	He gets on well with me.
Il se dispute rarement avec moi.	He rarely argues with me.
Il a le sens de l'humour.	He has a sense of humour.
Il a le sens pratique.	He is very practical.
Il a beaucoup d'imagination.	He is very imaginative.
Il a beaucoup d'enthousiasme.	He is very enthusiastic.
Il est capable de garder un secret.	He can keep a secret.
Il est un bon copain.	He is a good friend.

CREDIT

Top Tip
In the first lot of sentences, note how the object **me** comes before the verb, unlike in English ('He understands **me**.').

The next example features a girl you don't see eye to eye with for a number of reasons.

Elle m'énerve.	She annoys me.
Elle m'agace.	She irritates me.
Elle me critique.	She criticises me.
Elle ne me fait jamais confiance.	She never trusts me.
Elle s'entend mal avec moi.	She gets on badly with me.
Elle se dispute tout le temps avec moi.	She always argues with me.
Elle a mauvais caractère.	She is bad tempered.

CREDIT

Extended grammar

CREDIT

To further expand your descriptions of how people are, you will want to talk about what they have done in the past. For this you will need to use the *passé composé*. (See **Tenses 3** on pages 90–93.)

*Mon amie Sylvie, est très sociable: par exemple, le week-end dernier, elle **est allée** à une surprise-party avec ses copines et après, elle **a invité** des amies à ...*

My friend Sylvie, is very sociable: for example, last weekend she went to a surprise party with her friends and afterwards she invited her friends to ...

Think about examples you could give to back up your descriptions of people. Here are some ideas:

Il est généreux.	*Il m'**a donné** de l'argent de poche.*
Il est bruyant.	*Il **a joué** sa musique trop fort.*
Il m'énerve souvent.	*Il **a pris** mes baskets.*
Elle est compréhensive.	*Elle **a écouté** à mes problèmes.*
Elle est autoritaire.	*Elle **n'a pas écouté** mon point de vue sur ...*
Elle m'encourage beaucoup.	*Elle m'**a aidé** avec mes devoirs de maths.*

Top Tip
Use the vocabulary on pages 60–61 to help you work out the meaning of these sentences.

As you see, it's important to be sure of the *passé composé* in this topic.

The main points to remember are:

- Does the verb take *avoir* or *être*?

Il a parlé à mon ami.	He talked to my friend.
Il a acheté des chocolats.	He bought some chocolates.
Il a lu ma lettre.	He read my letter.
Il est allé en ville.	He went into town.
Il est venu me chercher.	He came to collect me.
Il est sorti avec ma sœur.	He went out with my sister.

- If the verb takes *être*, the past participle needs to agree when the subject is feminine.

Elle est sortie avec mon copain.
  She went out with my friend.
Elle est allée au cinéma avec lui.
  She went to the cinema with him.
Elle est partie de la maison.
  She left the house.

Quick Test

Make a list of five good and five bad qualities of a male or female friend or acquaintance in the present tense. Then, next to each one, write an example of what they have done recently to prove your point – in the past tense, of course!

Quick Test C

Work out whether these sentences are positive or negative, and put a + or a – next to each. Then translate them into English, if you can!

1 *Il me fait confiance.*
2 *Elle m'agace.*
3 *Elle s'entend bien avec moi.*
4 *Il a le sens de l'humour.*
5 *Il est un bon copain.*
6 *Elle a mauvais caractère.*
7 *Il n'a pas beaucoup d'enthousiasme.*
8 *Elle me critique.*

Relationships 3

Exercise 1

Sort these adjectives into two columns, POSITIVE and NEGATIVE.

Label each one **m** (for masculine) or **f** (for feminine).

Top Tip

For further practice, give the other gender of each adjective. Be careful – some don't change at all!

aimable	bruyante
désobéissant	sensible
malhonnête	créative
adorable	méchant
intelligente	paresseuse
ennuyeux	respectueux
indépendent	ordonnée
calme	passionnante

Exercise 2

13 Read through and listen to these two letters to Tante Amélie.

Note down the various problems of each person, giving as much detail as possible.

Chère Tante Amélie ...

Je vous écris parce que j'ai un grand problème chez moi! D'un côté, je m'entends vraiment très bien avec ma mère, puisqu'elle est généreuse tout le temps. Par exemple, nous sommes allées faire du shopping le week-end dernier, et elle m'a acheté une belle paire de chaussures et une robe pour une soirée. En plus, elle est souvent prête à m'aider: lorsque j'ai des ennuis avec mes devoirs de maths, elle m'aide beaucoup, car elle était douée en maths, je suppose!

Mais ce qui est bien, c'est qu'elle me comprend. L'année dernière, mon petit ami m'a quittée pour une autre fille, et j'ai pu tout discuter avec ma mère.

Mais mon beau-père, c'est quelqu'un de différent! D'abord, il est toujours trop autoritaire. Il m'a défendue de porter mon jean à l'anniversaire de Jules (mon nouveau copain). Le samedi passé, je suis rentrée tard à la maison (à une heure du matin, je crois) et il a été très fâché. Il est souvent en colère avec moi! Et quand je lui ai expliqué que j'allais quitter le lycée pour chercher du travail au supermarché, il a critiqué ma décision! Quel culot!

Que dois-je faire?!

Marianne

Chère Tante Amélie ...

Pourriez-vous m'aider, s'il vous plaît? Je suis en difficulté au lycée. Les autres garçons de mon âge ne s'intéressent qu'aux jeunes filles dans ma classe et cherchent sans cesse à se disputer avec les professeurs. Moi, j'ai horreur de ceux qui osent répondre comme ça aux profs. Ce qui m'intéresse surtout, c'est les maths et les sciences nats, pas la musique 'rap' avec ses paroles vulgaires et les chanteurs qui crient.

Tout le monde se moque de moi. L'autre jour, je suis entré dans la salle de classe en écoutant un peu de Mozart sur mon walkman, et tout de suite les élèves ont ri comme des fous. Vraiment, je trouve ça inacceptable! Mercredi dernier, j'essayais de réviser pour un contrôle de philosophie et il y avait des filles qui chuchotaient à côté de moi dans la bibliothèque. Quand je leur ai demandé de se taire (car c'est les règlements, vous savez), elles m'ont répondu que réussir aux examens ne leur disait rien. Imaginez quel avenir elles auront!

Veuillez m'aider, ma Tante Amélie, car je ne sais pas ce que je dois faire!

Vincent

Top Tip
Use the vocabulary from pages 60–61 to help you with the comprehension of these letters. This is also a good exercise for dictionary practice, especially with verbs and adjectives. However, definitions don't always give you the *meaning* of the verb, so it is important to recognise *subject* and *tense* with all verbs in these letters

Quick Test c

Say whether these statements about Vincent's letter are true or false:

1 Vincent has problems at school. ☐

2 Vincent admires those who answer back in class. ☐

3 He loathes rap music. ☐

4 He mocks everyone else. ☐

5 Last Wednesday he was trying revise for an assessment. ☐

6 There was a fire in the library. ☐

i

Quick Test

Can you jot down a few sentences of advice in French from Amélie?

Health issues 1

Basic vocabulary

Body parts

la bouche	mouth
le bras	arm
la cheville	ankle
le cœur	heart
le coude	elbow
le cou	neck
la dent	tooth
le doigt	finger
le dos	back
l'épaule	shoulder
l'estomac	stomach
le genou	knee
la gorge	throat
la jambe	leg
la langue	tongue
la main	hand
le nez	nose
l'œil (les yeux)	eye (eyes)
l'oreille	ear
l'orteil	toe
la peau	skin
le pied	foot
la poitrine	chest
le sang	blood
la tête	head
le ventre	stomach

Ailments

la blessure	injury
le bleu	bruising
la brûlure	burn
la constipation	constipation
la coupure	cut
la diarrhée	diarrhoea
la douleur	pain
la fièvre	fever, temperature
le gonflement	swelling
la grippe	flu
l'indigestion	indigestion
l'insolation	sun-stroke
la maladie	illness
le mal de mer	sea-sickness
la piqûre d'insecte	insect bite / sting
le rhume	a cold
la température	temperature

Quick Test C

Put these body parts in order, from head to toe:

Le cou

Le nez

L'orteil

La poitrine

L'épaule

La bouche

Le ventre

La jambe

Extended vocabulary

At the chemist's

l'aspirine	aspirin
la brosse à dents	toothbrush
le cachet	tablet
le comprimé	tablet
le cotton hydrophile	cotton wool
la crème	cream
la cuillerée	spoonful
le dentifrice	toothpaste
le médicament	medicine
l'ordonnance	prescription
le pansement	dressing, plaster
la pastille	throat lozenge, cough sweet
la pharmacie	chemist's
le pharmacien	chemist
la pilule	pill
le rasoir	razor
le savon	soap
le shampooing	shampoo
le sparadrap	plaster
la tube	tube

Doctor's / hospital / dentist's

l'accident	accident
l'ambulance	ambulance
l'assurance	insurance
l'attestation du médecin	doctor's certficate
le cas d'urgence	emergency
le chirurgien	surgeon
la consultation	consultation
le dentiste	dentist
le docteur	doctor
les frais	cost, expenses
l'infirmière	nurse
l'opération	operation
le patient	patient
le plombage	filling
la piqûre	injection
le remède	remedy, cure
le rendez-vous	appointment
la salle de consultation	consultation room
la salle d'attente	waiting room

Quick Test

Label this picture of a chemist's with the vocabulary you have learnt above.

One world 1

Basic vocabulary

Countries, continents, *la francophonie*

l'Europe	Europe
l'Afrique du nord	North Africa
l'Afrique du sud	South Africa
l'Amérique du nord	North America
l'Amérique du sud	South America
l'Asie	Asia
l'Australasie	Australasia
les pays francophones	French-speaking countries
la Francophonie	French-speaking countries
l'Algérie	Algeria
les Antilles	French West Indies
la Belgique	Belgium
le Cambodge	Cambodia
le Cameroun	Cameroun
le Canada	Canada

le Congo	Congo
la Côte d'Ivoire	Ivory Coast
la France	France
la Guinée	French Guinea
le Laos	Laos
le Luxembourg	Luxemburg
le Maroc	Morocco
Madagascar	Madagascar
la Martinique	Martinique
la Maurice	Mauritius
le Monaco	Monaco
le Nigeria	Nigeria
le Québec	Quebec
le Ruanda	Rwanda

le Sénégal	Senegal
la Suisse	Switzerland
le Tchad	Chad
la Tunisie	Tunisia
Zaïre	Zaire

People
Nationalities

les Algériens	Algerians
les Belges	Belgians
les Canadiens	Canadians
les Français	French
les Marocains	Moroccans
les Suisses	Swiss
les Tunisiens	Tunisians

Continental / race

les Africains	Africans
les Arabes	Arabs
les Européens	Europeans

Religions / status

les chrétiens	Christians
les catholiques	Catholics
les juifs	Jews
les musulmans	Muslims
les immigrés	immigrants
les immigrants	immigrants
parler …	to speak …
français	French
arabe	Arabic
créole	Creole

Quick Test

Read through these newspaper headlines and note down the English equivalent:

1 *Désastre naturel sur l'île tropicale*

2 *Inondation après la saison des pluies*

3 *Habitants dans les Alpes: la vie à l'altitude*

4 *Maladie en Afrique du sud: le SIDA attaque*

Extended vocabulary

Geography

les Alpes	Alps
l'altitude	altitude
la capitale	capital
la catastrophe	catastrophe
le climat	climate
le désastre naturel	natural disaster
le désert	desert
le fleuve	river
les habitants	inhabitants
l'île tropicale	tropical island
l'inondation	flood
la Méditerrannée	Mediterranean
la mer	sea
les montagnes	mountains
l'océan	ocean
l'Océan Atlantique	Atlantic Ocean
l'Océan Indien	Indian Ocean
l'Océan Pacifique	Pacific Ocean
la pluie	rain
la saison des pluies	rainy season
la sécheresse	drought
la terre	earth
le tremblement de terre	earthquake

Lifestyle issues

l'amour	love
l'attitude	attitude
l'alimentation	food
l'aliment de base	basic diet / food
la connaisance	knowledge

les différences culturelles	cultural differences
les différences culinaires	culinary differences
les différences religieuses	religious differences
l'école	school
l'éducation	education
l'enseignement	education
les enfants	children
la haine	hatred
la honte	shame
l'ignorance	ignorance
la langue (maternelle)	(native) language
la maladie	disease
le mode de vie	way of life
le monde	world
la moralité	morality
la mort	death
la naissance	birth
la nation	nation
la nationalité	nationality
la pauvreté	poverty
le pays d'origine	country of birth
le racisme	racism
la religion	religion
le respect	respect
la richesse	wealth
le SIDA	AIDS
le système scolaire	school system
le taux de mortalité	mortality rate
la Terre	Earth
le tiers-monde	Third World
la valeur	(moral) value

ⓘ Quick Test

Label the French-speaking countries in this map – in French, of course!

One world 2

Basic grammar

The most important aspect of this topic is gaining an awareness of the way of life in francophone countries. Since most of what you read and hear will concern the routine situations of those living in *les pays francophones*, you need to focus on the present tense. The *on* and *ils* forms are particularly useful here, as you will use them to talk about people in general.
(See **Tenses 1** on pages 84–6.)

Learn phrases using the following regular *–er* verbs:

acheter	to buy		**habiter**	to live
apporter	to bring		**manger**	to eat
arroser	to water	CREDIT	**parler**	to speak
cultiver	to grow		**pêcher**	to fish
creuser	to dig		**tomber**	to fall
dévaster	to devastate		**travailler**	to work
élever	to breed		**voler**	to steal
gaspiller	to waste			

Top Tip

Notice the endings on regular *-er* verbs in the present tense:
on → *–e*
ils → *–ent*
Both endings are silent.

On **achète** / Ils **achètent** du matériel pour l'école.	They buy equipment for school.
Le fleuve Niger **apporte** de l'eau au village.	The River Niger brings water to the village.
On **arrose** / Ils **arrosent** leurs légumes.	They water their vegetables.
On **cultive** / Ils **cultivent** des aubergines.	They grow aubergines.
On **creuse** / Ils **creusent** de nouveaux puits.	They dig new wells.
Les tempêtes **dévastent** les villages.	The storms devastate villages.
On **élève** / Ils **élèvent** des bœufs et des chèvres.	They breed cattle and goats.
On ne **gaspille** pas / Ils ne **gaspillent** pas d'eau.	They don't waste water.
On **habite** / Ils **habitent** au milieu du désert.	They live in the middle of the desert.
On **mange** / ils **mangent** du couscous, le plat traditionnel de l'Afrique du Nord.	They eat couscous, the traditional North African dish.
On **parle** / Ils **parlent** créole.	They speak Creole [a language created by the mixing of a native language and an introduced one, such as English or French].
On **pêche** / Ils **pêchent** tous les jours.	They fish every day.
Les pluies **tombent** en averses violentes.	Heavy rains fall.
On **travaille** / Ils **travaillent** toute la journée.	They work all day long.
On **vole** / Ils **volent** les troupeaux (de chameaux).	They steal herds (of camels).

Extended grammar

To expand your range of language in this topic, you'll also have to be prepared on other verbs. The most useful are listed below: note that these don't have the same endings as regular *–er* verbs.

aller	to go
apprendre	to teach
connaître	to know (a person / place)
construire	to build
détruire	to destroy
entretenir	to look after, keep
vendre	to sell
vivre	to live

On **va** / Ils **vont** *à l'école à pied.*	They go to school on foot.
On **apprend** / Ils **apprennent** *le Coran.*	They teach the Koran.
le livre sacré des musulmans	the Muslim scriptures
On **connait** / Ils **connaissent** *le paysage.*	They know the countryside.
On **construit** / Ils **construisent** *les toits.*	They build roofs.
On **détruit** / Ils **détruisent** *les forêts.*	They destroy forests.
On **entretient** / Ils **entretiennent** *les bateaux.*	They look after the boats.
On **vend** / Ils **vendent** *leurs poulets au marché.*	They sell their chickens at the market.
On **vit** / Ils **vivent** *de la terre.*	They live off the land.

Quick Test

Write out the sentences above with the verbs omitted. Have a break for five minutes (go and make a cup of tea!), then try to fill in the gaps with the appropriate verbs.

Quick Test

Join the two sides together to make a full sentence:

a	*le fleuve Niger apporte*	**1**	*à l'école à pied*
b	*les pluies tombent*	**2**	*sans cesse au mois de juillet*
c	*on construit*	**3**	*les toits en été*
d	*les enfants*	**4**	*de l'eau au village*

One world 3

Exercise 1

17

Read through and listen to this interview about what a typical French person eats. Think about how the reality matches what you know about French eating habits. You will find some useful vocabulary for this exercise on pages 54–55.

What, in your opinion, is typically or not typically French about Luc's diet? State your case!

A Alors, Luc, pour le petit déjeuner je suppose que tu prends des croissants tous les matins, c'est bien ça?

B Mais non, pas du tout! De temps en temps, le dimanche, peut-être, mais certainement pas pendant la semaine! Non, je mange du pain-grillé avec de la confiture!

A Et à boire? Du café?

B Non, c'est mauvais pour l'estomac. D'ailleurs, je n'aime pas tellement le goût. Moi, je préfère le thé.

A On dirait un vrai Anglais? Et à midi, qu'est-ce que tu manges?

B Alors, au lycée, heureusement, nous avons deux heures pour le déjeuner. Mais quand même je mange assez vite. Je vais en ville avec mes copains et on achète des frites chez McDo …

A Oh, là là! C'est affreux, ça!

B Oui, oui, je sais, et c'est très malsain, comme dit ma mère!

A Et avec ça? Les frites, ça remplit, mais pas pour longtemps …

B Effectivement … je mange aussi un paquet de chips ou même un yaourt.

A Mais je suppose que pour le dîner, vous mangez en famille …

B Oui, mais attends. Puisque j'arrive à la maison vers cinq heures et j'ai vraiment faim, tu sais, je prends une tartine et une barre de chocolat …

A Et le dîner c'est à quelle heure, donc?

B Ouf! Ça dépend, tu sais … Si papa est là, on mange tous ensemble, vers huit heures, mais autrement, ma mère ne prépare rien de spécial. Tout le monde se sert. Chacun prend ce qu'il lui plaît.

A Mais, si vous êtes tous là, que mangez-vous?

B Le plus souvent, pour commencer, du pâté ou de la soupe. Et après, comme plat principal, du bœuf avec des haricots verts ou des petits pois.

A Qu'est-ce que tu bois, d'habitude?

B Mais du coca, bien sûr! Ou bien du Irn Bru … c'est extra, ma sœur a passé quinze jours avec sa corres à Glasgow et on ne buvait que ça!

A Mais tu n'es pas typiquement français, toi!

Quick Test C

Make a list of what Luc actually eats and drinks at mealtimes, as opposed to what the interviewer presumes!

Exercise 2

18 — Read through and listen to this account of a visit to Marrakech, a city in Morocco.

Je me rappelle d'un séjour qu'on a passé quand j'avais sept ou huit ans au Maroc. Mon père était homme d'affaires et il voyageait assez souvent au nord de l'Afrique, car il était commerçant de textiles et il visitait des usines là-bas.

Nous avons logé dans un petit hôtel pas loin du centre-ville de Marrakech, qui est la ville la plus intéressante du Maroc, je crois. D'abord, la belle mosquée, la grande place et bien sûr les souks, c'est à dire les marchés où l'on vendait de tout: des souvenirs pour les touristes, évidemment, mais aussi des objets d'art, des épices, vraiment de tout. Mon père a acheté un chapeau en cuir. Moi, j'étais complètement ahuri et j'ai gardé des souvenirs très vifs de cette expérience.

La vieille ville de la médina était entourée d'un énorme mur. C'était très impressionnant!

En dehors de la médina, on trouvait le quartier moderne de Marrakech, qui était complètement différent, mais qui gardait aussi sa qualité exotique, arabe. Autour de la place étaient des cafés, des restaurants, des boutiques charmantes et toujours occupées, jour et nuit. On jouait de la musique traditionnelle le soir, le centre-ville était plein de monde, des taxis qui klaxonnaient sans cesse. D'autres amuseurs publics venaient, comme des conteurs, des charmeurs de serpents, bien sûr, que ma mère trouvait effrayants … Mais quel spectacle pour un gosse de mon âge!

Go over this piece again, concentrating on *tense*. Try to identify the tense of each verb: *passé composé* (for events and actions) or imperfect (for descriptions)?

Next find the French for these phrases:

Passé composé:

1 a short holiday we spent
2 we stayed in a small hotel
3 my father bought a leather hat
4 I've kept very vivid memories

Imperfect:

1 my father was a businessman
2 he used to travel quite a lot
3 markets where they sold everything
4 they played traditional music
5 it made a strong impression
6 when I was seven or eight

Try this activity again after you've worked through the section on Past tenses!
(See **Tenses 3** on pages 90–93.)

Glossary

se rappeler de – to recall
un séjour – a short stay / holiday
un homme d'affaires – a businessman
des usines – factories
la mosquée – Muslim place of worship
des épices – spices
en cuir – out of leather
ahuri – bewildered
un mur – a wall
en dehors de … – outside …
klaxonner – to honk your horn
sans cesse – non-stop
un gosse – a kid

Top Tip

Although the main focus of this account is tenses, it is also a very useful source of adjectives that you can use in your own work. Read it through again and note them down, looking up any you aren't sure of.

Tenses 1

Present tense

The present tense is used to talk about how things currently are or events that are happening now. This means that it is particularly important in the following topics:

- Self and family
- Relationships
- Likes and dislikes
- Describing where you live
- Typical holidays

- Friends
- Free time
- Routines at home
- What school is like, etc.

Whatever the tense, a systematic approach to learning verbs works best. This means identifying verbs by type. There are three types of regular verbs, with infinitives ending in –er, –ir and –re. (The infinitive is the form found in the dictionary, translated in English as 'to … '.)

Each type of regular verb has its own endings. The endings are different for each type, but once you learn the three patterns, you can use a lot of verbs!

–er verbs in the present tense

regarder	to watch		
*je regard**e***	I watch	*nous regard**ons***	we watch
*tu regard**es***	you watch (singular informal)	*vous regard**ez***	you watch (plural or formal)
*il regard**e***	he watches	*ils regard**ent***	they watch (all male or male / female mix)
*elle regard**e***	she watches	*elles regard**ent***	they watch (all female)
*on regard**e***	we / you / they watch		

The good news is that nearly all –er verbs go like this in the present tense (a notable exception is *aller* – to go, which doesn't follow these rules). Some useful ones follow here: these are worth memorising.

A *aimer* (to like), *adorer* (to love), *acheter** (to buy)

B *bavarder* (to chat)

C *chercher* (to look for), *changer* (to changer)

D *détester* (to hate), *donner* (to give), *durer* (to last)

E *écouter* (to listen), *espérer** (to hope)

F *fêter* (to celebrate)

G *gagner* (to earn, to win)

H *habiter* (to live)

I *influencer* (to influence)

J *jouer* (to play)

K *klaxonner* (to sound one's horn)

L *louer* (to hire, to rent)

M *manger* (to eat), *monter* (to climb)

N *nager* (to swim)

O *oublier* (to forget)

P *parler* (to talk), *porter* (to wear, to carry), *préférer** (to prefer)

Q *quitter* (to leave)

R *rentrer* (to go back), *retourner* (to return), *rêver* (to dream)

S *stationner* (to park)

T *tirer* (to pull, to shoot), *tomber* (to fall)

U *utiliser* (to use)

V *voyager* (to travel), *voler* (to steal) …

* Beware of accents changing!

(There aren't very many useful –er verbs right at the end of the alphabet …)

Top Tip
It's worth really getting to grips with the pronoun forms and meanings here: you'll need them throughout the tenses section.

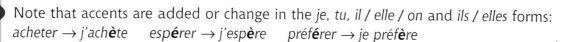

Note that accents are added or change in the *je, tu, il / elle / on* and *ils / elles* forms:

acheter → *j'ach**è**te*   *esp**é**rer* → *j'esp**è**re*   *pr**é**f**é**rer* → *je pr**é**f**è**re*

Note that when verbs such as *aimer*, *adorer* and *détester* are followed by another verb, the second verb is in the infinitive:

*J'aime **aller** en ville.*	I like going into town.
*Vous adorez **chanter**!*	You love to sing!
*Ils détestent **lire**, les enfants!*	The children hate to read!

–ir verbs in the present tense

finir	to finish		
*je fin**is***	I finish	*nous fin**issons***	we finish
*tu fin**is***	you finish	*vous fin**issez***	you finish
*il / elle fin**it***	he / she finishes	*ils / elles fin**issent***	they finish
*on fin**it***	we / you / they finish		

You'll find a lot of verbs ending in *–ir* have some kind of irregularity. You just have to learn these as you go along.

–re verbs in the present tense

attendre	to wait, to expect		
*j'attend**s***	I wait	*nous attend**ons***	we wait
*tu attend**s***	you wait	*vous attend**ez***	you wait
il / elle attend	he waits	*ils / elles attend**ent***	they wait
on attend	we / you / they wait		

Again, a lot of the useful *–re* verbs are not entirely regular. Learn the exceptions as you go along.

Irregular verbs

There is also a large group of *irregular* verbs. These don't follow the same patterns as any of the three main verb types, but they include some of the most common French verbs. It is very important to be able to use these accurately. Here are some of the most useful.

aller	to go		
je vais	I go	*nous allons*	we go
tu vas	you go	*vous allez*	you go
il / elle va	he / she goes	*ils / elles vont*	they go
on va	we / you / they go		

avoir	to have		
j'ai	I have	*nous avons*	we have
tu as	you have	*vous avez*	you have
il / elle a	he / she has	*ils / elles ont*	they have
on a	we / you / they have		

être	to be		
je suis	I am	*nous sommes*	we are
tu es	you are	*vous êtes*	you are
il / elle est	he / she is	*ils / elles sont*	they are
on est	we / you / they are		

Top Tip
Organising vocabulary grammatically and / or alphabetically as done here can really help you in memorising it.

Model folios 2

Sample essay 2 CREDIT

20

Les grandes vacances

J'aimerais vous parler de mes grandes vacances. D'habitude, tous les ans, on passe les grandes vacances chez nos cousins qui habitent à Inverness, une grande ville dans le nord de l'Écosse. On s'entend bien et il n'y a pas de disputes car nous avons les mêmes intérêts – par exemple, nous aimons faire des tours en vélo et sortir le soir en ville.

Mais l'année dernière, nous avons fait quelque chose de différent: nous sommes allés à Séville en Espagne et c'était absolument fantastique! Nous avons passé quinze jours dans cette ville charmante et historique, où nous avons logé dans un petit hôtel de luxe pas loin du centre. Le premier jour, nous sommes allés dans un bon restaurant typiquement espagnol et j'ai essayé la spécialité régionale (du poulet avec une sauce piquante et des pommes de terre) – il faut dire que la nourriture était délicieuse. On a visité les cathédrales et les monuments historiques, qui étaient un peu ennuyeux à mon avis! Mais après cela, on a acheté des souvenirs pour nos copains en Écosse – ma petite sœur a choisi un t-shirt vraiment touristique et moi, j'ai acheté des CDs de musique pop espagnole.

Tous les matins, quand il ne faisait pas encore trop chaud, on se promenait dans les jardins publics. Mais un jour, ma mère est tombée malade parce qu'elle est restée trop longtemps au soleil. Pourtant, les grandes vacances étaient une bonne expérience et j'ai envie maintenant de retourner en Espagne! Et vous, avez-vous passé des bonnes vacances?

238 words

Top Tip

Read through and listen to this essay on summer holidays. Try to think of a short title for each of the three paragraphs. This will help you to focus on how the writer has structured his response to what could have been a very limited idea.

How good is this essay?

This is an excellent essay – a clear grade 1. It has many strengths, showing a good range of tense, being very accurate and including a wide variety of expressions.

Its main strength, however, is that it contains many extended sentences, developing an idea or including an example. It is not difficult to do this in your writing and speaking, but it is surprising how few such extended sentences you find in Standard Grade folios! If you want your work to stand out, it's a good idea to work on features like this.

Quick Test

Find as many examples of the following in the essay as you can:
- pronouns
- holiday topic nouns (places, food items, shopping)

How to prepare for folio assessments

Here are some suggestions only:

- Organise your essay into clear sections: introductory line(s) – first paragraph – second paragraph – concluding line(s).
- The introduction only needs to explain the title in a single full sentence.
- The first paragraph can deal with one side of the title, or one point of view. Be sure you know which tense(s) are needed.
- The second paragraph deals with the other aspect of the title, or the other point of view. This is a good chance to show you can talk about things in another tense.
- The conclusion is often best when it poses a couple of questions to the reader, as this wraps up what you have to say and turns towards the reader. Questions are also tricky in French, so this would demonstrate your ability to ask them!

Once you have considered the structure and contents, write it out. In the lead up to the assessment date in class, bear the following in mind:

- Hand it in on time, so that the teacher's comments on your draft can be followed through.
- Learn it by heart in sections.
- Test yourself at home and try using test conditions, e.g. no more than 40 minutes, dictionary only, etc.
- Go over this home-test: how accurate was it, when comparing it with your good copy? Did it suffer towards the end? Do you have to cut it down in order to have a consistent level of accuracy?
- Overuse of or over reliance on dictionaries can be a big problem – they should be used only to double-check spelling or meaning.

Some basic language

Numbers

0 zéro	31 trente et un	61 soixante et un	91 quatre-vingt-onze
1 un	32 trente-deux	62 soixante-deux	92 quatre-vingt-douze
2 deux	33 trente-trois	63 soixante-trois	93 quatre-vingt-treize
3 trois	34 trente-quatre	64 soixante-quatre	94 quatre-vingt-quatorze
4 quatre	35 trente-cinq	65 soixante-cinq	95 quatre-vingt-quinze
5 cinq	36 trente-six	66 soixante-six	96 quatre-vingt-seize
6 six	37 trente-sept	67 soixante-sept	97 quatre-vingt-dix-sept
7 sept	38 trente-huit	68 soixante-huit	98 quatre-vingt-dix-huit
8 huit	39 trente-neuf	69 soixante-neuf	99 quatre-vingt-dix-neuf
9 neuf	40 quarante	70 soixante-dix	
10 dix			100 cent
	41 quarante et un	71 soixante et onze	101 cent un
11 onze	42 quarante-deux	72 soixante-douze	200 deux cents
12 douze	43 quarante-trois	73 soixante-treize	300 trois cents
13 treize	44 quarante-quatre	74 soixante-quatorze	1000 mille
14 quatorze	45 quarante-cinq	75 soixante-quinze	2000 deux mille
15 quinze	46 quarante-six	76 soixante-seize	
16 seize	47 quarante-sept	77 soixante-dix-sept	
17 dix-sept	48 quarante-huit	78 soixante-dix-huit	
18 dix-huit	49 quarante-neuf	79 soixante-dix-neuf	
19 dix-neuf	50 cinquante	80 quatre-vingts	
20 vingt			
	51 cinquante et un	81 quatre-vingt-un	
21 vingt et un	52 cinquante-deux	82 quatre-vingt-deux	
22 vingt-deux	53 cinquante-trois	83 quatre-vingt-trois	
23 vingt-trois	54 cinquante-quatre	84 quatre-vingt-quatre	
24 vingt-quatre	55 cinquante-cinq	85 quatre-vingt-cinq	
25 vingt-cinq	56 cinquante-six	86 quatre-vingt-six	
26 vingt-six	57 cinquante-sept	87 quatre-vingt-sept	
27 vingt-sept	58 cinquante-huit	88 quatre-vingt-huit	
28 vingt-huit	59 cinquante-neuf	89 quatre-vingt-neuf	
29 vingt-neuf	60 soixante	90 quatre-vingt-dix	
30 trente			

Time

Days

lundi
mardi
mercredi
jeudi
vendredi
samedi
dimanche

Months

janvier
février
mars
avril
mai
juin
juillet
août
septembre
octobre
novembre
décembre

Seasons

au printemps	in spring
en été	in summer
en automne	in autumn
en hiver	in winter

Time

Il est …	It's …
une heure	1.00
deux heures cinq	2.05
trois heures dix	3.10
quatre heures quinze / et quart	4.15
cinq heures vingt	5.20
six heures vint-cinq	6.25
sept heures trente / et demie	7.30
huit heures trente-cinq	8.35
neuf heures quarante	9.40
dix heures quarante-cinq / onze heures moins le quart	10.45
onze heures cinquante	11.50
douze heures cinquante-cinq	12.55
… du matin	… in the morning
… de l'après-midi	… in the afternoon
Il est midi.	It's midday.
Il est minuit.	It's midnight.

Top Tip

Dates in French are simple: *le huit mai, le quatorze juillet,* etc. The only exception is the first of a month: *le premier janvier.*

Quick Test

The 24-hour clock: if 13.00 (treize heures) is 1.00 p.m., can you work out these other times in the 24-hour clock and then in French?

8.15 p.m.
9.30 p.m.
3.00 a.m.
7.10 a.m.

Answers

Personal Language

Self

Quick test (p. 13)

1 She is quite tall and slim.
2 I have brown hair and green eyes.
3 He is serious but amusing.
4 I am completely impatient.
5 My mother is really sensitive.

Exercise 1 (p. 16)

les cheveux roux – red hair
les yeux marron – brown eyes
les cheveux raides – straight hair
Je suis de taille moyenne. – I'm average height.
Je suis assez costaud. – I'm quite sturdy.
Je ne suis pas très fort. – I'm not very strong.
sympa – nice
sensible – sensitive
égoïste – selfish
J'ai quinze ans. – I'm 15.
Je suis anglais. – I'm English.
Je n'ai pas de frère. – I've no brothers.
J'habite Glasgow. – I live in Glasgow.
C'est dans l'ouest. – It's in the west.
Mon anniversaire, c'est le deux mars. – My birthday is
  on 2 March.
J'ai les yeux bleus. – I've got blue eyes.
J'ai les cheveux noirs. – I've got black hair.
Je suis assez petit et mince. – I'm quite small and thin.
Normalement, je suis amical. – I'm generally friendly.
Je suis rarement méchant. – I'm rarely mean.
Quelquefois je suis timide. – Sometimes I'm shy.

Quick Test (p. 17)

1 T	2 F	3 F	4 T
5 T	6 F	7 F	8 T

Family

Quick test (p. 21)

1e, 2f, 3a, 4d, 5c, 6b

Exercise 1 (p. 22)

mon frère	*mon grandpère*
ma demi-sœur	*mon copain*
ma petite amie	*mes parents*
sa mère	*sa tante*
son oncle	*ses copines*
ses amis	*ses grands-parents*

Male Jobs	Female jobs
programmeur	programmeuse
vendeur	vendeuse
professeur	professeur
secrétaire	secrétaire
directeur	directrice

Present	Imperfect	English
elle travaille	*elle travaillait*	she works / worked
il va	*il allait*	he goes / went
ils habitent	*ils habitaient*	they live / lived
il est	*il était*	he is / was
ils ont	*ils avaient*	they have / had
ma mère joue	*ma mère jouait*	she plays / played
ils travaillent à l'étranger	*ils travaillaient …*	they work / worked

Exercise 2 (pp. 22–23)

Family member	Age	Physical description	Character	Job	Other details
grandfather	89	very tall, thin, long grey beard, big moustache	generous	director bank	Victor
grandmother	82	very pretty		model, dancer	Marie-Antoinette Romanian
father	60	quite tall; short curly hair	nice, understanding	businessman	Gérard
mother	born 1958	pretty, brown eyes, long brown hair	sensitive, charming; sense of humour / joker, practical	actress	Eloise, born in Spain

Quick test (p. 23)

Marie-Antoinette – b   Gérard – a, c   Eloise – d, e

Hobbies

Quick test (p. 25)

1 comics and historical novels
2 TV films
3 plays guitar with friends
4 He also listens to the radio in the mornings.

Exercise 1 (p. 28)

je fais   je vais   on joue   on fait   j'aime
elle préfère   elle collectionne   je trouve

Exercise 2 (p. 28)

1 *les romans d'aventure*
2 *je fais du karaté*   3 *je rentre*
4 *au volley*   5 *jeux électroniques*

Quick test (p. 28)

2 *de temps en temps*
3 *le mercredi*
4 *souvent*

Education

Quick test (p. 33)

a 2	b 8	c 1	d 4
e 6	f 5	g 7	h 3

Exercise 1 (p. 34)

1   3
2   3
3   English and Spanish
4   Wednesday is free to allow pupils to practise religion
5   French
6–8   own response

Quick test (p. 34)

1 *sœur*	2 *récré*
3 *devoirs*	4 *professeur*

Exercise 2 (p. 35)

Sandrine: **1** F **2** T **3** F **4** T **5** F
Lény: **1** T **2** T **3** F **4** F **5** F

Where I live

Quick test (p. 39)

1 You can walk in the park.
2 I want to visit the historical sights.
3 Tourists can go shopping at the shopping centre.
4 Are you sporty? You can go to a good rugby match.

Exercise 1 (p. 40)

petite, l'ouest, voir, pied, sportif, rugby, après-midi, sport, été, pratiquer, de fond

Exercise 2 (pp. 40–41)

The grumpy old man comes from **Gornac** in the south-west of France.
Gornac is **100 kilometres** from Bordeaux. It has only 73 inhabitants, and **English** and German tourists in the summer. There's **no disco**, but there is a **youth club** where they play **chess** in winter. There's even a cup-winning **football** side!

Quick test (p. 41)

1 yes	2 no
3 no	4 no
5 no	6 yes
7 yes	

Tourist Language

Transport

Quick test (p. 43)
1 *composteur*
2 *passage souterrain*
3 *carnet*
4 *consigne automatique*
5 *horaire*

Quick test (p. 45)
1 by ferry
2 London
3 By car
4 William, his penpal

Exercise 2 (p. 47)
composter	to stamp your ticket
gare routière	bus station
camion	lorry
horaire	timetable
salle d'attente	waiting room
voyageurs	travellers
vol	flight
tarif supplémentaire	extra cost
correspondance	(travel) connections

Exercise 3 (p. 47)
1 train from Nîmes arriving at platform 5 in 10 minutes
2 Air France flight 307 for London 1 hour late
3 next train to Paris will leave from platform 12b at 21.35
4 buffet to close at 23.00 tonight
5 for passengers on Nice express train: this train is direct
6 a British passport has been handed in to Lost Property
7 due to poor weather and fog, flight to Moscow delayed for 2 days. All passengers to Air Flot desk now!

Quick test (p. 47)
1 present, 2 past, 3 past, 4 past, 5 present or future, 6 present, 7 past

Holidays

Quick test (p. 51)
1 You should leave your key at reception.
2 You should return before 10 p.m.
3 Clients should pay deposits immediately.
4 Boys should tidy dormitories every morning.

Exercise 1 (p. 52)
MANAGER *Bonjour, monsieur. Que puis-je faire pour vous?*
TOURIST *Je m'appelle Henri Martin. J'ai fait une réservation pour une chambre.*
MANAGER *Je ne trouve pas de réservation à ce nom …*
TOURIST *Mais j'ai réservé la chambre il y a un mois!*
MANAGER *Nous avons une chambre libre …*
TOURIST *Où se trouve la chambre?*
MANAGER *Votre chambre est au troisième étage.*
TOURIST *L'ascenseur est en panne?*
MANAGER *Oui, monsieur. Prenez l'escalier!*
TOURIST *La chambre est trop bruyante – elle donne directement sur la rue principale!*
MANAGER *Je regrette, monsieur, c'est la seule chambre disponible!*
TOURIST *La douche ne fonctionne pas.*
MANAGER *Je vais téléphoner immédiatement au plombier.*
TOURIST *Le petit déjeuner est compris?*
MANAGER *Ah non, monsieur, je regrette encore, mais le petit déjeuner est supplémentaire.*

Exercise 2 (p. 53)
1 boys not allowed on 3rd floor
2 no smoking
3 no football in dorms
4 no eating in hall or lounge
5 no singing in toilets or showers after 9 p.m.

Eating out

Quick test (p. 55)
STARTER	MAIN COURSE	VEG	CHEESE	DESSERT
4	5, 6	2, 8, 9	1	3, 7, 10

Quick test (p. 57)
1 c – Is service included?
2 c – I didn't order this dish.
3 w – How would you like your steak?
4 c – I would like to see the manager.
5 c – What's the dish of the day?
6 w – We're full.

Exercise 1 (p. 58)
drinks
vin	wine
orangina	Orangina
citron pressé	squeezed fresh lemon juice
express	espresso
chocolat	hot chocolate

snacks
crêpe	pancake
sandwich au fromage	cheese sandwich
glace	ice-cream
pizza	pizza
croque-monsieur	toasted cheese and ham sandwich
chips	crisps

Exercise 2 (p. 59)
Below are the English translations, for reference:
A table for how many?
Which menu are you having?
Have you chosen yet?
And to drink?
How would you like your steak done?
Would you like to order a sweet?
Where in Scotland do you come from?
Have a nice day!

Exercise 3 (p. 59)
1 Table 5: lamb chop and roast chicken – €11,50
2 Table 12: 2 espressos, 1 vanilla ice – €3,10
3 Table 6: 2 mussels, 1 pizza, 1 jug of white wine – (no price given)
4 Table 15: 1 steak and chips, 1 mixed salad, 1 soup of the day, 1 sauerkraut, 2 beers, 1 mineral water, 1 coke – €23,70
5 Table 4: 6 snails, 1 veal, 1 bottle red wine – €16,50

Quick test (p. 59)
deux cafés au lait	*trois thés citron*
un jus d'ananas	*un café crème*
trois sandwichs au jambon	*deux glaces vanille*
un croque-monsieur	*un sandwich au pâté*
une crêpe confiture	*deux cocas*
une crêpe citron	*une eau gazeuse*

Problems

Relationships

Quick test (p. 61)

1 mother is hardworking, but not always reasonable
2 little brother is mature, but too chatty
3 elder sister is artistic, but self-centred
4 father is a laugh, but sometimes too loud

Quick test (p. 63)

1 He trusts me. (+)
2 She annoys me. (–)
3 She gets on well with me. (+)
4 He has a sense of humour. (+)
5 He is a good friend. (+)
6 She has an unpleasant personality. (–)
7 He is not very enthusiastic. (–)
8 She criticises me. (–)

Exercise 1 (p. 64)

Positive

aimable (m/f)   sensible (m/f)   créative (f)   adorable (m/f)
intelligente (f)   respectueux (m)   indépendent (m)   ordonnée (f)
calme (m/f)   passionnante (f)

Negative

bruyante (f)   désobéissant (m)   malhonnête (m/f) méchant (m)
paresseuse (f)   ennuyeux (m)

Health issues

Quick test (p. 66)

Le nez
La bouche
Le cou
La poitrine / l'épaule
Le ventre
La jambe
L'orteil

Quick test (p. 68)

1 I've got the 'flu
2 She is constipated
3 Have you got a temperature?
4 He has a sore stomach.
5 I'm hot!
6 Are you thirsty?
7 My grandfather is dead / has died / died
8 She has backache

Environment

Quick test (p. 75)

1 In my opinion, there is quite a lot of noise in big towns / cities.
2 I think that there is less exhaust emission nowadays.
3 According to the government, we do not have enough protection against pollution.

Exercise 1 (p. 76)

1 Claire
2 Thomas
3 Simon
4 Thomas
5 Simon
6 Claire

Exercise 2 (pp. 64–65)

Letter 1 – Marianne

• step-father too authoritarian
• didn't allow her to wear jeans to boyfriend's birthday
• was angry when she returned late last Saturday
• often angry with her
• criticised her decision to leave school to look for supermarket job

Letter 2 – Vincent

• pupils argue with teachers
• he likes studying; other boys interested only in girls
• other pupils listen to rude rap music; he likes Mozart and when he listens to it, they laugh at him
• last Wednesday he was trying to revise for a philosophy test and was disturbed by girls whispering in the library

Quick test (p. 65)

1 T
2 F
3 T
4 F
5 T
6 F

Exercise 3 (pp. 70–71)

1 He calls her 'mister'!
2 Sunbathing recklessly
3 He thinks the boy has broken his arm.
4 He imagines that the boy has hurt his ankle in a bike accident.
5 He and his wife visited Scotland 20 years ago.
6 The boy has a temperature of 40 degrees; he has sunstroke from sunbathing all day
7 Two pills before each meal, with a glass of water
8 Go to the chemist's!

Quick test (p. 71)

Face

La bouche (mouth)
Les dents (teeth)
Les lèvres (lips)

Body

Le ventre (stomach)
Le doigt (finger)
Le dos (back)
La cheville (ankle)
Le genou (knee)

Exercise 2 (p. 77)

Isabelle

Country +ve: life simpler; more tranquil; feel closer to nature; lots to do – fish in lake, etc.
Town –ve: very polluted; noisy; too much traffic; never safe at night

Martin

Country +ve: pure air; picturesque; nature is looked after; can appreciate species which are endangered elsewhere
Country –ve: mountains very boring; nothing for young people; can't get about easily – friends live in next village, so rarely see them

Quick test (p. 77)

rendre visite à – to visit
se sentir – to feel
s'amuser – to enjoy oneself
trouver – to find / consider
apprécier – to appreciate

One world

Quick test (p. 78)

1 Natural disaster on tropical island
2 Floods after the monsoon season
3 The inhabitants in the Alps: life in altitude
4 Disease in South Africa: AIDS-attack

Quick test (p. 81)

a4   b2   c3   d1

Quick test (p. 82)

Toast with jam
Tea
Macdonald's meal chips
Crisps
Yoghurt
Slice of bread and jam (tartine)
Chocolate bar
Pâté
Soup
Beef
Green beans
Peas
Coke
Irn Bru

Exercise 2 (p. 83)

passé composé

on a passé   nous avons logé   mon père a acheté   j'ai gardé

imperfect

j'avais   mon père était   il voyageait   il était   il visitait   on vendait
j'étais   la médina était   c'était   on trouvait   qui était   qui gardait
étaient des cafés   on jouait   qui klaxonnaient
d'autres amuseurs publics venaient
ma mère trouvait

passé composé phrases to translate:

un séjour qu'on a passé
nous avons logé dans un petit hôtel
mon père a acheté un chapeau en cuir
j'ai gardé de souvenirs très vifs

imperfect phrases to translate:

mon père était homme d'affaires
il voyageait assez souvent
les marchés où on vendait de tout
on jouait de la musique traditionnelle
c'était très impressionnant
quand j'avais sept ou huit ans

Writing and Speaking

Tenses 1

Quick test (p. 86)

1 – aime
2 – habites
3 – finit
4 – attendons
5 – finissez
6 – aiment

Tenses 2

Quick test (p. 88)

1b	2c	3a
4e	5f	6d

Model folios 1

Quick test (p. 95)

present

s'appelle
se situe
c'est x 2
est x 3
je suis
je prépare
tu as

conditional tense

j'aimerais / je voudrais écrire / rester / continuer / aller

Model folios 2

Quick test (p. 97)

pronouns

on   nous   je / j'   il   elle

holiday topic nouns

les vacances d'été
les tours en vélo
quinze jours
un bon restaurant
du poulet
des pommes de terre
les cathédrales
des souvenirs
le soleil
une bonne expérience
une grande ville
Espagne
un petit hôtel de luxe
la spécialité régionale
la sauce piquante
la nourriture
les monuments historiques
les jardins publics
les grandes vacances

Some basic language

Quick test (p. 99)

8.15 p.m.	20.15	vingt heures quinze
9.30 p.m.	21.30	vingt et une heures trente
3.00 a.m.	3.00	trois heures
7.10 a.m.	7.10	sept heures dix

Index